Its *All* Inside

A Thought Exchange Workbook for Sourcing
Success and Happiness From the Inside Out

by David Friedman

Published by:
Library Tales Publishing, Inc.
www.LibraryTalesPublishing.com
www.Facebook.com/LibraryTalesPublishing

For general information on our other products and services, please contact our Customer Care Department at 1-800-754-5016, for technical support, please visit www.LibraryTalesPublishing.com

Library Tales Publishing also publishes its books in a variety of electronic formats. Every content that appears in print is available in electronic books.

ISBN-13: 978-0999275832
ISBN-10: 0999275836

PRINTED IN THE UNITED STATES OF AMERICA

TABLE OF CONTENTS

INTRODUCTION
"THINK POSITIVE" - EASIER SAID THAN DONE

We all know that "positive" Thoughts lead to a "positive " Experience of life, so why is it that we have so much trouble holding onto our "positive" Thoughts? We choose a "positive" Thought, and in no time at all we find ourselves thinking our old "negative" Thoughts again. It can't be that we're lazy or stupid. There must be a good reason why this happens.

It was this question that inspired me to come up with the concept of The Thought Exchange®, over a decade ago. Since that time, it has been my mission to help people to not only choose the Thoughts they wish to think, but perhaps even more importantly, to be able to stay with those Thoughts and Experience the results they produce.

I have written two books on the subject, *The Thought Exchange - Overcoming Our Resistance to Living a Sensational Life* and *The Healing Power of Negative Thoughts and Uncomfortable Sensations - Stop Being Afraid of Them and Start Using Them to Heal"* in which I explain, in great detail, the principles of Thought Exchange, and offer anecdotes and examples to support the work.

Over the years, many people have asked me when I was going to come out with a book that compiled, in readily accessible form, all the Exercises and Meditations contained in those two books, as well as others that I taught in workshops all over the country. This is that book.

After a brief explanation of what The Thought Exchange® is, followed by some definitions of terms you'll need to know in order to understand what I'm talking about, I offer, in this book, a series of Exercises and Meditations that you can do anytime, anywhere, even if you haven't studied my other books or taken my workshops. Of course, if these Exercises should spark an interest in you in learning more about The Thought Exchange®, my two other books should tell you everything you might want to know about it. At the end of each section of Exercises, I have included references to specific pages in my other books where you can find more detailed information on the particular subject the section covers.

WHAT IS
THOUGHT EXCHANGE?

Thought Exchange is a method of breaking through the blocks to our choosing and sticking with the Thoughts we wish to hold.

When we think a Thought, we experience Sensations in our body. Thoughts cause Sensations. If, in our childhood, or even in the more recent past, a particular "positive" Thought (and our expressing it to someone) was met with punishment or physical or emotional abuse, if we try to take on that "positive" Thought today, we may feel the same physical discomfort we felt as a child. As defenseless children, we quickly figured out that when we thought (and expressed) that Thought, we felt "uncomfortable." So we learned to make ourselves more "comfortable" by making sure we never thought that Thought again. The trouble is, by doing this, we have set up a circumstance where these "positive" Thoughts are now inaccessible to us.

When we try to take on one of the "positive" Thoughts that got us in trouble, we feel "uncomfortable," and immediately jump to a "negative" Thought to "protect" ourselves from this discomfort.

As soon as we think and express a "negative" Thought, people will often say, "Don't be so negative!"

So we try to take on the "positive" Thought again.

But the moment we do that, we feel "uncomfortable," and we jump back to the "negative" Thought.

Which leads us to results we don't want, so we try to take on the "positive" Thought again.

But this, once again, makes us "uncomfortable," so we jump back to the "negative" Thought.

And 'round and 'round we go.

The Sensations that we felt in our childhood, which meant that we were in danger then, are harmless now that we're adults. In Thought Exchange, we learn to be with the discomfort that comes with a particular Thought we want to hold, and by being able to do this, we develop the ability to take on, and stay with, any Thought. Like a dancer's feet hurting, or a performer whose heart pounds before he or she goes on stage, these Sensations just become an accepted part of holding the Thought we wish to hold, and we get to do what we want to do and be what we want to be.

Simple. But not easy.

Often these Sensations are very powerful, and bring up strong memories and resistance. But revealing these Sensations for what they really are, harmless relics from the past, has a twofold benefit. Not only does it give us the freedom to choose any Thought (In Thought Exchange we don't say, "Change" a Thought, we say, "Exchange" one Thought for another; all Thoughts are available to us at all times") but by being with these Sensations that our "Inner Child" could not tolerate, we heal our Inner Child and become more integrated beings, with constant access to the unlimited possibilities that MUST exist at ALL times.

HOW TO USE THIS BOOK

Unlike many "Self-Help" programs, Thought Exchange is not about "getting rich quick" or "seeing all your worldly dreams and desires manifest." Thought Exchange is about what goes on in the place you REALLY live, on the Inside, in the world of your own Experience. Unlike the illusory "outer" world in which temporary physical manifestations come and go, sometimes satisfying us for the moment, sometimes not even doing that, the Inner World is where Everything ALWAYS exists, where Infinite Possibility is a constant, ever-present reality, and is the only place where Peace, Happiness and Fulfillment can ever be found.

When we truly examine why we want anything in the "outside" world, it always boils down to our wanting to feel a certain way: feel safe, feel proud, feel fulfilled, etc. Thinking that something in the "outside" world will cause these things to happen in the "inside" world is putting the cart before the horse. In fact, it is only when we can recognize that we already have these things in the "inside" world that we will begin to see them in the "outside" world in a way that truly satisfies us.

Make no mistake about it. When you are able to choose the Thoughts you wish to think and are able to be with the Sensations that arise when you think those Thoughts, you WILL see the Manifestations you desire. (You will also desire the Manifestations you see.)

The Exercises in this book are designed to give you the Experience of the Infiniteness that you actually are. As such, they progress in a specific order, and should be done in the order in which they're presented in this book. Sometimes the Exercises will not seem to produce immediate changes. Sometimes you'll wonder why you are doing them. Sometimes several Exercises may seem to be saying the same thing. Sometimes you will not understand what you are doing. Some of the Exercises are to be done for the moment, and some are to be done over a long period of time.

What we're going for are both subtle and profound changes in where and how we experience our lives, and we can only get there in stages. Basic concepts must not only be understood, they must be Experienced. So hang in there with the Exercises, and as much as you can, just do them without worrying about why, how, what for, or what results you are getting. If you do them, they will get you to Experience yourself as the Being you truly are; Infinite, Powerful, Joyous, Free, Safe and Creative.

Once you have taken yourself through all the Exercises, you may, of course, feel free to return to those that have particularly resonated with you, or to those that pertain to a particular situation in which you find yourself. But, if you can, try to go through the whole book, as this will cause a basic shift in the way you hold yourself and the world that will allow any exercise you go back to to be more effective.

Once you've done this, the contents of this book will be embedded in your Subconscious. If you have a particular Exercise you want to return to, of course go to it. But if you just want to get some piece of wisdom and you don't know what it is you need, simply open the book to any page and trust that your Subconscious will take what you land on and use it for exactly what it is you need at that moment.

NOTE: This book contains unusual capitalizations of words and quotation marks around certain words. I capitalize a word if it represents a concept that has a unique definition in Thought Exchange. So you will find words like Thought, Sensation, Experience and others capitalized throughout the book. I put quotation marks around words that, because we live only in the world of our interior Experience, are matters of opinion rather than Truths. So words like "positive," "negative" and "uncomfortable" have quotation marks around them. I also write a number of words in ALL CAPS, like EVERYTHING, MUST and REALLY for emphasis in certain contexts.

After a section defining Thought Exchange terms, the Exercises are divided into sections by subject:

I. DEFINITIONS

Thought Exchange has specific terminology that you need to understand in order to grasp the concepts. In this section, I define all the terms you need to know.

II. IT'S ALL INSIDE

In order to practice Thought Exchange, you must be aware of where you actually Experience life and who you REALLY are. These Exercises are designed to help you Experience that. Some of them may seem counter-intuitive or you may not understand exactly why you're doing them. We're going for a real change in consciousness and orientation in the world, so if you can, just do the Exercises on Faith and get whatever you get. They will make more sense later. (If you want more information on why you're doing these or what they mean, you can find it in my two other books, *The Thought Exchange* and *The Healing Power of "Negative" Thoughts and "Uncomfortable" Sensations*.)

III. THE TECHNIQUE OF THOUGHT EXCHANGE

The Exercises in this section will teach you how to use the techniques of Thought Exchange to choose the Thoughts you wish to hold, be with and Experience the Sensations that go with them, and by doing this, create the Experience of life you wish to create.

IV. MANIFESTATION EXERCISES

Once you truly understand that Manifestation is nothing more than a reflection of your Internal Experience, and have learned, through the preceding exercises, to work with your Internal Experience, you can use Thought Exchange as a tool to manifest what you wish to see in the world. In Truth, when your Thoughts and Inner Experience are where you want them to be, things will automatically manifest as effortlessly as your reflection in a mirror appears when you stand in front of it. The mirror has no choice. It MUST reflect what is in front of it.

V. HEALING YOUR INNER CHILD

The Exercises in this section deal with healing your past by healing your Inner Child. Through doing these Exercises, you will learn to integrate the past and the present, to take care of your Inner Child while acting as an Adult in the present, and to reparent your Inner Child by truly getting to know and Experience it, perhaps for the first time.

VI. SOLVING "PROBLEMS"

The exercises in this section deal with solving "Problems," both those that come up on a daily basis and those that concern long-term issues like Health, Relationship and Money. In Thought Exchange, "Problems" are not bad things. They are mirrors which, if used properly, ALWAYS guide us to greater Mastery and internal Peace and Power.

VII. THE HIGHER POWER WITHIN YOU

Once you understand that EVERYTHING is ONLY happening inside of you, in the world of your internal Experience, and that Infinite Possibilities ALWAYS exist inside of you, these Exercises will help you reach inside yourself for the answer to every question, as opposed to reaching outward.

APPENDIX: THOUGHT EXCHANGE PRINCIPLES IN REVIEW

This section contains a listing of over 100 Basic Principles and Ideas that are covered in the Exercises in this book. Reading through the list regularly, or whenever you feel stuck or confused, can serve as a way to remind yourself of who you REALLY are and what you're REALLY capable of.

So, as my partner, Rev. Shawn Moninger likes to say, "Put on your hardhats. We're going in!"

PART I
DEFINITIONS

Certain terms have a specific meaning when referred to in Thought Exchange. Here is basic terminology that you may need to fully understand the Exercises that follow.

Thought - A Thought is an image in your mind. It can come in pictures or in words. It is invisible. You can think ANY Thought. You can think, "I am fabulous." You can think, "I am terrible." You can think, "I am a success." You can think, "I am a failure." (You don't have to Believe a Thought to be able to Think it. It's important that we know this, because it frees us to be able to think ANY Thought we wish to think.) We can imagine ANYTHING. "A purple elephant; being a billionaire; breathing on the moon." (Even if you think there's no possible way you could breathe on the moon, you CAN still imagine it.) No Thought is objectively true or false. No image is objectively possible or impossible. A Thought is only a matter of opinion, based on what you Experience inside yourself. Different people will think different Thoughts in the same circumstances. None of them are right or wrong. They're just thinking Thoughts.

Sensation - A Sensation is something you physically Experience in your body. Like a Thought, it is invisible. It is an Experience. A Sensation is not a Feeling. Anger, Sadness, Love, Joy are not Sensations. They are Feelings. Sensations are things like Pain, Tingling, Itching, Hotness, Coldness, Tightness, Pounding (not the actual pounding of, say, your heart, but how you Experience that Pounding.) We often avoid Sensations, jumping immediately to Thoughts about them. But simply being with our Sensations is the core of Thought Exchange work. Sensations, like Thoughts, intrinsically have no meaning. We interpret them by thinking about them, in essence making up erroneous stories about what they mean, and this often gets us into trouble.

Belief - A Belief is a Thought that we think is true. Since

no Thought is actually true, a Belief takes one Thought, which is a part of the whole, and says that it IS the whole. For example, a Belief might be, "I NEVER fail." This Belief leaves out all the Possibilities of failure, which must, of course, still be there, no matter what we believe. So a Belief is, in effect, a lie, because it limits Possibilities to only the ones you want to see, or are afraid to see. We take on Beliefs because we want to see something in a particular way, or because we want to protect ourselves from entertaining certain Possibilities that make us "uncomfortable." When the Belief works for us, that's great. But, "I ALWAYS fail" is also a Belief that many people take on, and if that's what they Believe, that's what they will see. (The funny thing is, even when they succeed, if they are holding the Belief "I ALWAYS fail, their success will be Experienced within that Belief. That's why so many people who we would call extremely successful continue to Experience themselves as failures.) You can't Exchange a Belief directly, because inherent in a Belief is that you think it's true. In order to Exchange a belief, you must first recognize that it's just a Thought. Then you can Exchange it for any other Thought, and when you are able to be with the Sensations that that new Thought produces, that new Thought will become a new Belief. If you are holding a Belief you like, there's no desire or need to Exchange it. If you are holding a Belief that's holding you back, you can recognize that that Belief is just a Thought, and then Exchange it for another Thought that you prefer to hold.

Feeling - What we typically call Feelings are actually Thoughts about Sensations. Often, when we ask someone what Sensations they are feeling, they will tell us what Thoughts they are thinking about the Sensations. For example, if someone says, "I'm angry" and I say, "How do you know you are angry?" they will say something like, "I have a hotness in my chest." A hotness in your chest can be interpreted as many things; Passion, Discomfort, Warmth, An-

3

ger. A hotness in your chest is nothing more than a hotness in your chest. In Thought Exchange, we learn to focus on the understanding that a Sensation is intrinsically meaningless, rather than on the meaning we assign to it with our Thoughts. In this way, unlimited Possibilities remain open to us, because no matter what Sensations we're experiencing, unlimited possible Thoughts are always available to us.

"Protective" Thought - When we take on a "positive" Thought and that Thought produces an "uncomfortable" Sensation that we think we can't tolerate, we will jump away from that "positive" Thought to a Thought that is the opposite. We do this in order to feel more "comfortable." People often call these Thoughts "negative" or "self-sabotaging" Thoughts, but in Thought Exchange we call them "protective" Thoughts, because they protected our Inner Child from pain it couldn't tolerate which was associated with a "positive" Thought the Inner Child took on. There's good reason why we, as children, took on these "protective" Thoughts. When we can understand this, we don't criticize ourselves or beat ourselves up, but rather, empathize with ourselves and with our Inner Child.

Inner Child - In the context of Thought Exchange, our Inner Child is the child we were when we had traumatic events happen to us that went unprocessed. Like the soldiers on Japanese Islands who, twenty years after World War II ended, did not know that the war was over and were still hiding and braced for an attack, the Inner Child is still living in its trauma and in its interpretation of it. The Inner Child makes itself known by generating "negative" Thoughts and "uncomfortable" Sensations in our present Adult mind and body. Everything that happens to us is not only reacted to by us as Adults, but by our Inner Child as well. Frequently, these two reactions are very different, and this can be extremely confusing to our Adult self, because we can't understand why we would be upset about things that as an

4

Adult we shouldn't be upset about. People often feel that the reactions of the Inner Child are in their way, and try to push their Inner Child aside, get rid of it, overcome it, or tell it to shut up. But since the Inner Child is a part of us, it cannot be gotten rid of, and must be heard, seen and felt in order for us to become whole. Since the Inner Child lives in our body, we are the ONLY ones who can do that for the Inner Child. It doesn't help to tell the Inner Child that "It's OK now," because the Inner Child doesn't live in the "Now." It lives in the "Then." What the Inner Child needs is for the Adult to feel and recognize the Experiences the Inner Child had (and is still having), to hold and stay with the Inner Child by feeling what the Inner Child felt and is still feeling ("uncomfortable" Sensations) and to be able to stay with those "uncomfortable" Sensations and still take on Adult thoughts and perform Adult actions. Although the Inner Child is usually quite young, anything that happened before right now, even something that happened yesterday, can be labeled Inner Child if the event has not been seen, heard, felt and processed by our Adult self.

Manifestation - A Manifestation is something we see, temporarily, in the physical world. (Everything in the physical world is temporary.) When we "Manifest" something, we move it from the invisible world (where it always MUST be and always MUST eternally exist as one of an Infinite number of Possibilities) to the physical world where we are able to temporarily "see" it.

"The Great Unmanifested" - Everything ALWAYS exists in the invisible world of Infinite Possibilities. When a songwriter "writes" a song, that particular combination of words and music already exists, always has existed, and always will exist in the Invisible World. In the "writing" of the song, the writer temporarily brings the song into physical Manifestation. When the song is sung, it temporarily exists in the Physical World. As soon as it's not being sung, it goes back into the Invisible World. But since we can remember that particular combination, we can always call it forth into Manifestation again by singing it. What we see in the finite Manifested world is an extremely tiny fraction of what exists in the Infinite Unmanifested world. And everything that exists in the Manifested world only exists there temporarily. Every song, every object, every building, every person, every planet, every star, is only visible temporarily in the Manifested world. But in "The Great Unmanifested," every possible thing (which is EVERY thing, no matter how far-fetched it might seem) is ALWAYS there, forever. So when we don't see something we would like to see in the Manifested world, we can always look into "The Great Unmanifested," find it (it's got to be there - anything you can imagine plus everything you can't imagine right now must be there) and begin the process of temporarily Manifesting it.

The Thought Exchange - The Thought Exchange is a store we made up to symbolize how Thought Exchange works. The store is open 24 hours a day, 7 days a week, it has every possible Thought in stock, and you can go in at any time and Exchange a Thought you're holding for any Thought you desire, no questions asked. You can Exchange a Thought you've held for fifty years and have worn out. You can come in a hundred times a day and Exchange the same Thought for another Thought. You can order by mail, by telephone or telepathically. It's ALWAYS there, ALWAYS open, and ALWAYS has every Thought in stock.

The Truth - The Truth is the way things are, what is possible (everything) and how the Universe works. The Truth is unchanging. There is no such thing as "My" Truth or "Your" Truth. There is definitely such a thing as "My" opinion or "My" Thought. But what we think at any given moment does not change the Truth. The Truth is that Infinite Thoughts, Infinite Possibilities and Infinite Manifestations are ALWAYS available to us.

"Positive" Thought - A "positive" Thought says that something is possible. It opens up the idea that something can be found in "The Great Unmanifested," that something you desire can be achieved, that something you think of as good is available to you. And since the Truth is that EVERYTHING can be found in "The Great Unmanifested," it must also be true that it is possible for ANYTHING to be achieved. Thus a "positive" Thought is a reflection of the Truth. When you take on a "positive" Thought, it sometimes comes with "uncomfortable" Sensations, and this is the principle reason why we often don't take on "positive" Thoughts, and don't stay with them when we do take them on. If you can be with the "uncomfortable" Sensations that arise when you take on a particular "positive" Thought, the Thought will become a Belief (a thought you think is true) and you will see the world through the lens of that "positive" Belief, no matter what happens.

"Negative" Thought - A "negative" Thought is one that limits possibility or, to be more specific, negates a possibility that actually is there. A "negative" Thought isn't bad or wrong, it just says that something isn't there or isn't possible. As such, a "negative" Thought is not a reflection of the Truth, since the Truth is that everything MUST be there and MUST be possible. Sometimes "negative" Thoughts protect us from pain, but they also limit us from Manifesting our Unlimited Possibilities. A "negative" Thought can always be Exchanged for a "positive" Thought, but in order to stay with that "positive" Thought, we have to be able to tolerate any "uncomfortable" Sensations that might come up when we think the "positive" Thought.

Impossible Double Bind - An Impossible Double Bind is a circumstance in which there is no solution which is safe or comfortable. It is often the Impossible Double Binds we

7

were put in as children that caused us to have to take on "protective" Thoughts. An example of an Impossible Double Bind would be something like the common abusive parental expression, "Stop crying or I'll give you something to cry about!" The child is in pain, but is told that if it expresses its pain it will get hit more, so it tries to not express its pain which means no one sees its pain and it remains in pain. Pain either way. An impossible double bind. Or the Pavlovian example, where a bell was rung every time a dog was about to get fed, and then when the dog reached for the food, the dog was given a shock. In very short order, the dog stopped reacting to the bell. The dog was in an Impossible Double Bind. It was hungry but would get shocked every time it reached for food. "Learned Helplessness" is often the result of being in an Impossible Double Bind for any length of time.

"The Mirror of the World" - Our whole life takes place inside us, in the world of Experience. When we look out at the world, what we're really seeing is Our Thoughts, Our Sensations, and Our Experience. We don't cause the world to happen, we see Ourselves in it. This is important to know, because just as when you're unhappy with an outfit you see in the mirror you change the outfit on Yourself (you would be insane to try and change the mirror) so when you see something you don't like in the world, you must turn to your Own Thoughts, Sensations and Beliefs in order to see a change. And when you do see a change, the change you're seeing is in You, not in the world, no matter how much it appears to be "outside" you. (Just as there is nothing in a mirror but a reflection of You.)

Observer/Noticer/Experiencer - Who we actually are is an invisible Observer/Noticer/Experiencer, located nowhere and unaffected by any Thoughts, Sensations or "outside" world" events we might be Observing/Noticing/Experiencing. So it could be said that who we are is "Nothing, located

Nowhere." This one can be difficult to understand, but it is crucial to our being able to Experience our Infiniteness, our Safety, and our Comfort in the world. There are Exercises in the Exercise section of this book that will allow you to truly Experience and get comfortable with this basic concept.

Experience - Experience is the sum total of what goes on inside us. So Experience is made up of our Thoughts and Sensations being Observed by our Observer/Noticer/Experiencer.

PART II
It's ALL Inside

Our lives happen 100% inside ourselves, in the world of our Experience. This is the ONLY place in which we experience life, and hence, the ONLY place in which we actually live.

EXERCISE 1
Experiencing, On The Inside, An Incident That Has Happened

Sit quietly with your eyes closed.

Think about an incident, something that's happened. Recall it in as much detail as you can.

Notice that with your eyes closed, this incident is "happening" inside of you, in the world of your Experience.

EXERCISE 2
Experiencing, On The Inside, An Incident That Has Not Happened

Sit quietly with your eyes closed

Make up an incident that didn't actually happen and think about it.

Think about this incident in great detail. (You are making up the details.)

Notice that with your eyes closed, this incident is "happening" inside of you in the same way as an incident that actually did happen. Your Inner Experience is equally real, whether the incident actually happened or not.

EXERCISE 3
Noticing Where You REALLY Experience Things

With eyes open, look at an object in the room. Although that object appears to be "out there," in Truth the ONLY way you register that object is as an image on your own retina in your own eye. The object is registering inside of you, and as it does, you have Thoughts about the object and you Experience "physical" Sensations when you look at the object. See if you can Notice and Experience that.

See if you can wrap your mind around the fact that ALL you know is that something is registering inside of You. Entertain the possibility that this very same "object" or color or incident might register differently inside someone else. In fact, I like to say, when I'm speaking to a group of people, "I can't prove that you are even here. All I know is that I see you. But if I were dreaming, I would also see you, just as 'real' as I see you now." We can't prove that anything we see is really there, but we can KNOW that something is there in our Experience, because we are Experiencing it.

See if you can experience that EVERYTHING that is "happening" is ONLY happening inside of You. If you can't get there yet, just entertain the possibility.

EXERCISE 4
Noticing Your Thoughts

Close your eyes and Notice your Thoughts. Whatever you are thinking, simply Notice it. If you are having trouble Noticing any Thoughts at all, notice that you are having the Thought that you are having trouble Noticing your Thoughts. Your Thoughts may keep changing. You may stay on one Thought. There is no right way to do this. Just Notice that you are having Thoughts.

13

EXERCISE 5
Noticing Your Sensations

Now notice any physical Sensations you are having in your body. By Sensations, I do not mean Feelings, like Anger, Sadness, Love, Fear. I mean "physical" Sensations, like Tingling, Itching, Hotness, Coldness, the Sensation of Pounding (not whatever it is that's causing that Sensation i.e. your heart or blood rushing, but rather the Experience of the Sensation itself), Tightness, Shakiness, etc. Just be with the Sensations. Notice that different parts of your body may be having different Sensations. Notice that the Sensations you're having may keep changing or may stay the same. Notice that you may have a desire to get away from some Sensations: some may feel "uncomfortable," some "comfortable." Just practice staying with your Sensations, whatever they are. If you notice yourself drifting away from them, gently bring yourself back to them. There's no right or wrong way to do this. Just Notice your Sensations.

EXERCISE 6
Thoughts and Sensations are ALL we Experience

Now, with eyes closed, Notice your Thoughts and Sensations at the same time. If that's too difficult to do, go back and forth between Noticing your Thoughts and Noticing your Sensations. See if you can Experience that these are the ONLY Experiences you are having right now, and in fact, the only Experiences you can ever possibly have. There is NO OTHER WAY you Experience other than Thoughts and Sensations. Thoughts and Sensations are 100% of our Experience.

EXERCISE 7
Noticing Who's Noticing

Close your eyes.

Notice your Thoughts. Whatever they are, whether they keep changing or remain the same, or even if you think you can't find any (that's a Thought too) just focus on your Thoughts and notice them.

Now shift your focus to noticing your Sensations. Notice any physical Sensations you're having: Hotness, Coldness, Tingling, Tightness, Itching, whatever. Notice that you may be having different Sensations in different parts of your body. Notice that your Sensations may keep changing or may stay the same. Just notice your Sensations.

Now shift back to noticing your Thoughts. Then, after a few moments, shift back to your Sensations, and keep switching back and forth, noticing Thoughts, Sensations, Thoughts, Sensations, etc.

Now......Notice Who Is Noticing all this! Who is it that is Noticing all these Thoughts and Sensations. It can't be the Thoughts and Sensations themselves. Something, or Someone, is Noticing them. See if you can Notice and Experience that there is an Invisible Consciousness, a "You" that is just "Here", but doesn't exist in physical time and space.

Ask yourself, "How do I know I exist?" and you will Experience a Consciousness, an Experience of Being. This invisible YOU, Noticing/Observing/Experiencing Thoughts and Sensations, is who you REALLY are. You are NOT the Thoughts or Sensations themselves. Don't worry if it's difficult to wrap yourself around this idea. Just keep doing the Exercise.

EXERCISE 8
Experiencing Yourself as the Observer/Noticer/Experiencer (ONE)

Close your eyes.

Notice your Thoughts.

Notice that you're Noticing them.

Notice the difference between the Thoughts and the Observer/Noticer/Experiencer that is Noticing them.

See if you can Experience yourself as the Observer/Noticer/Experiencer, located nowhere, non-physical, that is Experiencing Thoughts. They're not even "your" Thoughts. They're just Thoughts being Experienced, floating on through if you will.

Notice that who You are, the Invisible Observer/Noticer/Experiencer, has no Thoughts. Who YOU are is just looking at them.

If you Notice Thoughts like, "I can't do this; I am my Thoughts; I can't find this," or any other "negative" Thoughts, see if you can Notice that these are not the Thoughts of the "Observer/Noticer/Experiencer but rather Thoughts that the "Observer/Noticer/Experiencer is Observing/Noticing/Experiencing.

Now, repeat the same process with your Sensations.

Notice your Sensations.

Notice that you're Noticing them.

Notice the difference between the Sensations and the Observer/Noticer/Experiencer that is Noticing them.

See if you can Experience yourself as the Observer/Noticer/Experiencer, located nowhere, non-physical, that is Experiencing Sensations. They're not even "your" Sensations. They're just Sensations being Experienced, floating on through if you will.

Notice that who You are, the Invisible Observer/Noticer/Experiencer, has no Sensations, Who You are is just looking at them.

If you Notice Thoughts like, "I can't do this; I AM my Sensations; I can't find this," or any other "negative" Thoughts, see if you can Notice that these are not the Thoughts of the "Observer/Noticer/Experiencer.

If you Notice any Thoughts about Sensations, these are not the Thoughts of the Observer/Noticer/Experiencer. They are Thoughts that the Observer/Noticer/Experiencer is Noticing.

When you finish Noticing your Sensations, go to your Experience of being the Observer/Noticer/Experiencer and practice Noticing both Thoughts and Sensations, either at the same time, or switching back and forth from one to the other. Just sit there and Notice Thoughts and Sensations floating on through. Notice that they have nothing to do with the Observer/Noticer/Experiencer. They do not take anything away from the Observer/Noticer/Experiencer, nor do they add anything to the Observer/Noticer/Experiencer. They are just being Observed/Noticed/Experienced by the empty space located nowhere that is YOU.

Some people find this exercise very comforting and liberating. Others find it disconcerting. Just stay with it and allow yourself to Notice how it feels to Experience yourself as an Invisible Noticer, existing Nowhere in physical space.

EXERCISE 9
No Past, No Future, Only The Present

Think about something that happened in the Past. Notice that the ONLY place it now exists is in your Thoughts, Now, in the Present. If you're having Sensations around the Thoughts you're thinking about the Past, notice that those Sensations ONLY exist inside of you, in the Present. See if you can wrap yourself around the Experience that the Past doesn't exist, is nowhere to be found, cannot be found, and ONLY exists in the Present, Inside of You, in your Thoughts and Sensations. Period.

Now think about the Future. Notice that although it may seem like there IS a Future, like things ARE going to happen, the Future ONLY exists inside of You in Your Thoughts and Sensations in this moment. And in THIS moment, no matter what your Thoughts and Sensations are, Infinite possible outcomes MUST exist. There is no Future, there is nothing that exists at this moment that we could call the Future. There is ONLY the Present. And when you are in the Future, you will not be in the Future, you will be in the Present at THAT moment. See if you can wrap yourself around the Experience that the Future does NOT exist, except as Thoughts and Sensations in the Present.

So the next time, and every time you find yourself worrying about the Past or the Future, see if you can bring your Experience back to the only place it exists, which is within you, in the form of your Thoughts and Sensations at THIS moment, knowing that there is nothing to worry about concerning the Future or the Past, because THERE IS NO FUTURE OR PAST. Never was, and never will be.

EXERCISE 10
Experiencing The Truth of Who You REALLY Are

Now that you know that you are not your Thoughts and Sensations but rather the Observer/Noticer/Experiencer of them, let's Experience the qualities of who you REALLY are.

Close Your Eyes

Notice any Thoughts and Sensations your are having.

Notice that you are Noticing these Thoughts and Sensations.

Go to the invisible, located-nowhere, Experiential You that is Noticing Thoughts and Sensations, and see if you can experience that the Thoughts and Sensations are not part of the REAL You, but are merely being Noticed by the REAL You.

See if you can experience that this REAL You is completely empty. It doesn't think. It doesn't feel. It has no physicality. It just IS.

See if you can simply sit in this Nothingness. You'll probably see Thoughts and Sensations drifting by, being Observed, but see if you can just sit in this empty place. Some may find it scary, some comforting, but this place is who you REALLY are, and when you can really get yourself there, it is anything but scary. It's complete Peace, Serenity and non-verbal, Experiential Understanding. This is the "Meaning of Life." It can't be explained or understood or thought about. It can ONLY be Experienced.

EXERCISE 11
Your Body is NOT You

Close your eyes. Sit in the place of Observer/Noticer/Experiencer and become aware that that's who you REALLY are. Think about your body. Notice that with your eyes closed, the only way you know that your body is even there is by Thoughts (imagining your body) and Sensations (which you perceive to be in your body).

Notice that your body is being "created" in your Experience by the Thoughts and Sensations you're Observing/Noticing/Experiencing. See if you can get in touch with the idea that rather than your body creating your Experience, your Experience of your body is an outgrowth of the Thoughts you take on about the Sensations you Experience. By doing this Exercise, you gradually become aware that you are creating your body through the Thoughts and Sensations on which you focus your attention.

This Exercise is crucial in being able to deal with illness, weight issues, pain or any "discomfort" you might feel in your body. Rather than going to the body and trying to fix or change it, (which would be like asking a mirror to change without changing what's in front of it) we understand that who we REALLY are is an Infinite Consciousness located Nowhere, creating the Experience of our body by the particular Thoughts and Sensations, out of the Unlimited Possible Thoughts and Sensations that exist, on which we choose to focus.

Every time you see something in your body that you would like to change, take on a different Thought, and Experience whatever Sensations come with that New Thought, even if they're "uncomfortable." Stay with that New Thought, even if it seems to directly contradict what you're seeing in your body. When we learn to do this, we ultimately Experience that our body is nothing more than a reflection of our Thoughts. In this way, we attain Mastery over our body.

Our body is not who we are. It's just a reflection of our Thoughts, designed to show us what our Thoughts are, just as a mirror is only there to show us what we look like.

EXERCISE 12
You Are Safe

Part 1
Your Thoughts and Sensations
Do Not Affect Who You REALLY Are

Observing Your Thoughts and Sensations

Close your eyes

See if you can experience your True Self, your Observer/ Noticer/Experiencer as an enclosed Circle. You are the Emptiness, Nothingness inside that Circle.

Outside of the Circle are Thoughts and Sensations which you are simply Observing.

Notice that the Thoughts and Sensations cannot come into the Circle, but can only be seen by it. As such, the Circle never changes, its borders are never violated, and it never gains or loses anything because of Thoughts or Sensations.

Here's a drawing of what that looks like:

THOUGHT   SENSATION

YOU
OBSERVER/
NOTICER/
EXPERIENCER

SENSATION   THOUGHT

THOUGHT   SENSATION

Notice that You, as the invisible Observer/Noticer/Experiencer, are contained in the Circle, and all the Thoughts and Sensations are going on outside the Circle. Go to your Observer/Noticer/Experiencer and stare at this drawing from that place. See if you can Experience the sense that who you are is truly safe and unaffected by any Thoughts and Sensations that float around you.

Part 2
What Happens in the "Outside World"
REALLY Does Not Affect Who You REALLY Are

If the only way in which we ever Experience anything in the "outside" world is as Thoughts and Sensations within ourselves, and if who we REALLY are is an invisible, non-physical Observer of those Thoughts and Sensations, then who we REALLY are is, in essence, twice-removed, and thus twice-protected from anything that happens in the "outside" world.

Observing the "Outside" World

Close your eyes.

Think of something that has happened or is happening in the "outside" world.

Notice that the ONLY way that "happening" appears in You is in the form of Thoughts and Sensations.

See if you can Notice that in the ONLY place you can ever Experience anything (Thoughts and Sensations inside of You) the thing that is "happening" in the "outside" world is no longer, in your Experience, even "happening." It has been converted to Thoughts and Sensations. Since the ONLY thing you can ever Experience is Thoughts and Sensations inside yourself, you can't even know if anything is ever really "happening" in the outside world. All you can KNOW is that you are Experiencing Thoughts and Sensations.

Now go to your Observer/Noticer/Experiencer, Notice the Thoughts and Sensations that are being Experienced, and look way past them to the incident you originally thought of. Notice that you are not even Experiencing that incident. You are only Experiencing Thoughts and Sensations. That incident will seem a million miles away. See if you can Experience that that incident has no effect whatsoever on who you REALLY are. Here's a drawing of what this looks like. Notice that who you REALLY are is doubly removed and thus protected from any events that might occur in the world.

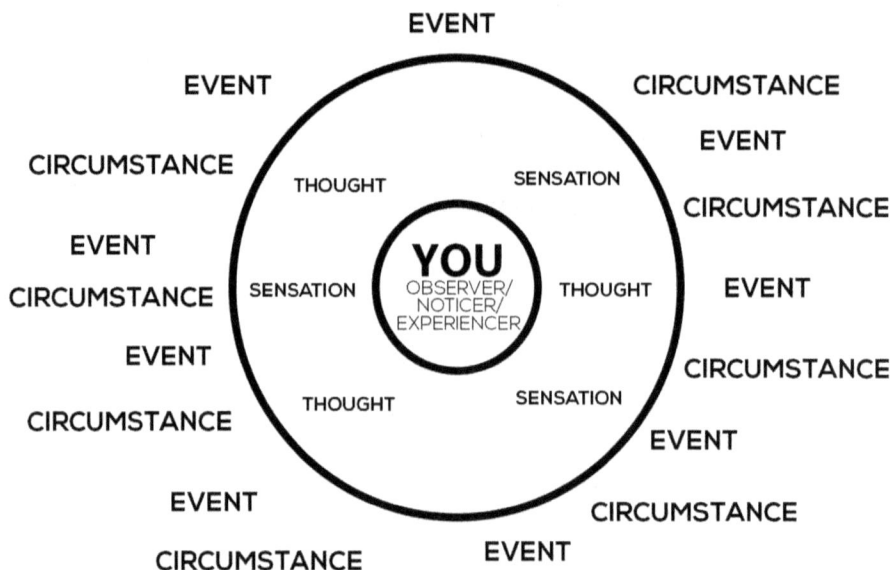

EVENT

EVENT   CIRCUMSTANCE

CIRCUMSTANCE   EVENT

THOUGHT   SENSATION

EVENT   CIRCUMSTANCE

CIRCUMSTANCE   SENSATION   **YOU**   THOUGHT   EVENT
OBSERVER/
NOTICER/
EXPERIENCER

EVENT   CIRCUMSTANCE

CIRCUMSTANCE   THOUGHT   SENSATION

EVENT   EVENT

EVENT   CIRCUMSTANCE

CIRCUMSTANCE   EVENT

EXERCISE 13
Pulling Back The Telescope

Whenever either events in the "outside world" or your Thoughts and Sensations feel too overwhelming, see if you can remind yourself of who you REALLY are by consciously receding into your Observer/Noticer/Experiencer and viewing those events from the "distance" this vantage point provides.

Notice how when you are able to do this, suddenly the events or Thoughts and Sensations have no effect on who you REALLY are.

24

EXERCISE 14
Experiencing "Oneness"

Close your eyes

Notice any Thoughts and Sensations you're having.

Align yourself with the Observer/Noticer/Experiencer.

Using the abbreviation for Observer/Noticer/Experiencer (ONE) repeat silently, "I AM ONE." (Actually, your Observer is not the one saying this. These words are being Observed, but this meditation can help you get closer to the experience of being ONE.

When we bring up the concept of all of us being ONE, this is what we really mean. All anyone is is an invisible Observer/Noticer/Experiencer, located-nowhere. Since the Observer/Noticer/Experiencer is non-physical and has no location, this is where we are all ONE. This is not "My" Observer, it's 'The" Observer: located Nowhere and Everywhere; containing Nothing and Everything: Infinite Possibility, cannot be endangered; cannot be changed; cannot be expanded; cannot be contracted; cannot be born; cannot die.

Chew on this concept in meditation. Civilization has chewed on it since time immemorial. Religions have been formed based on it. We have made up the word "God" to describe it, have created false images of "God" (IN TRUTH NO IMAGE IS POSSIBLE - "GOD" IS INVISIBLE AND EXISTS NOWHERE), put forth doctrines about Who "God" is (NOBODY) and where "God" is located (NOWHERE) and what gender "God" is (NONE) and how "God" will show "Himself" to us (CAN'T - "GOD" HAS NO PHYSICALITY AND IS LOCATED NOWHERE)

Wars have been fought in the name of "God," but in this invisible, located-nowhere place of ONE there could not be war, there could not be hatred, there could not be jealousy. All these "conditions" are only Observed from this place, but when we know that we are actually IN this place of ONE, that this is who we REALLY are, there is only Peace, Infiniteness and Possibility. There is only LOVE, the acceptance of all things as they are, because nothing can hurt us or even affect the I AM that we REALLY are.

See if rather than trying to figure anything out, you can simply Observe/Notice/Experience Thoughts and Sensations from this place of "ONE." In this exercise, do it by repeating, "I Am One" as you sit in the Experience of being the Observer/Noticer/Experiencer located nowhere. And let whatever images and conclusions about "God" form themselves from this place.

See if you can Notice that when you are aware that the REAL You is in this place, you feel connected to other people and events in a new and deeper way.

See if you can Notice that this place of Infinite Possibility, Infinite Safety and Infinite Connection to the riches of the entire Universe is not someone or something that you are praying to, but rather, it IS you.

For more detailed information on the subject of "It's All Inside," please refer to:
The Thought Exchange, pgs. 125-156
The Healing Power of "Negative" Thoughts and "Uncomfortable" Sensations, pgs. 1-19, 81-93

PART III
THE TECHNIQUE OF THOUGHT EXCHANGE

Now that we know that EVERYTHING is ONLY happening on the Inside, and that who we REALLY are is Infinite Possibility and Unassailable Empty Space, we are in a position to work on our lives in the place where they are really happening…. our Inner World of Experience, which is 100% made up of our being An Invisible Observer of Invisible Thoughts and Sensations. Period!

The Thought Exchange® is a technique designed to work with our Internal Experience rather than working with the "illusion" of the "outside" world. In doing this, we deal with our Thoughts and Sensations and the Unlimited Possibilities for Experience that they present. The result is that at any moment, no matter what is going on, we have the power to Experience true Unlimitedness, true Peace, true Choice, true Power and true Freedom. And the things we've wanted to Manifest, rather than being the goal, appear as reflections of who we already are inside.

The Thought Exchange Circle

In order to better understand the Exercises that follow, it's important to understand the principles on which Thought Exchange is based. This chart, and the explanation that follows, will give you all you need to know in order to get the most out of the Exercises.

NOTE: Before going on, it may be helpful for you to review the definitions of the terms; Thought, Sensation, Belief, Manifestation, Protective Thought, Inner Child, Mirror of the World and Experience, in the Definitions section of this book.

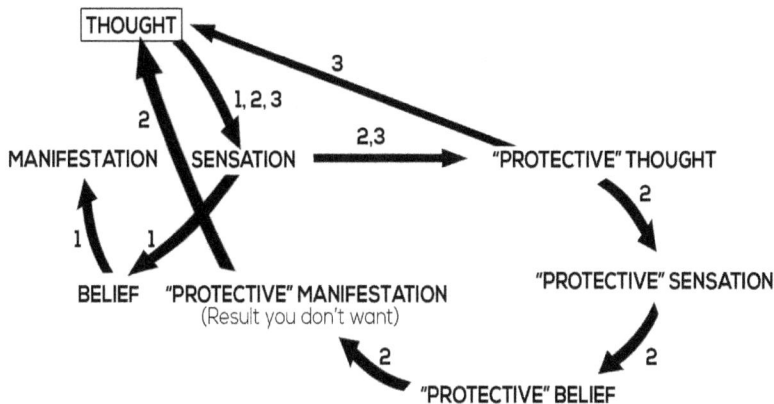

THOUGHT

3

1, 2, 3

2

2, 3

MANIFESTATION   SENSATION   "PROTECTIVE" THOUGHT

2

1   1

"PROTECTIVE" SENSATION

BELIEF   "PROTECTIVE" MANIFESTATION
(Result you don't want)

2   "PROTECTIVE" BELIEF   2

As you can see, when we take on a Thought we wish to hold, there are 3 paths that we can follow on this chart. Which path we follow is entirely our choice, but in order to follow the path that allows us to hold onto the Thought we wish to think, we have to, at times, be able to Experience and stay with "uncomfortable" Sensations.

Path 1

We think a Thought. If the Sensations the Thought generates are tolerable to us and we are able to be with those Sensations without having to run away from them, the Thought becomes a Belief, and we think the Thought is True. Our Belief will appear as Manifestation in the Mirror of the World before us. In other words, our Beliefs determine HOW we see whatever appears before us in the Mirror of the World. (NOTE: Our Beliefs do not necessarily determine WHAT we see before us, but rather HOW we see whatever is before us. And since our lives take place ONLY inside of ourselves, HOW we see things is the ONLY thing that is important.)

Path 2

We take on a Thought. If we are unable to be with the Sensations generated by the Thought we choose to hold, because we find them too "uncomfortable," we will "Exchange" that Thought for a Thought that produces less "uncomfortable" Sensations. We will Exchange our original Thought for a "protective" Thought. (Note: More often than not, the Thought that produces the "uncomfortable" Sensation is a "positive" Thought.)

This "protective" Thought (usually the opposite of our original Thought) will produce a Sensation that is more tolerable to us.

Because the Sensation produced by the "protective" Thought is more tolerable to us and we are able to stay with it, the "protective" Thought" now becomes a Belief, and as such, we think it's true.

Our new "protective" Belief" will appear as Manifestation in the "Mirror of the World" before us. We will see the world as the opposite of the original Thought we chose to take on, or, in simpler terms, as a result we don't want.

Realizing that we now see the world as the opposite of the Thought we originally took on, we will usually at some point, return to the original Thought, and will immediately, once again, go around the Circle. Whether we choose Path 1 or Path 2 depends on whether we can stay with the "uncomfortable" Sensations the "positive" Thought we take on produces.

Path 3

I call Path 3 the "shortcut" because it circumvents having to go all the way around the "Protective Circle" and just takes us directly back to the original "positive" Thought from the "protective" Thought. When we take on a "positive" Thought, feel an "uncomfortable" Sensation, and notice that we have Exchanged our "positive" Thought for a "protective" Thought, we can immediately Exchange the "protective" Thought back for the "positive" Thought and take another run at being with the "uncomfortable" Sensations the "positive" Thought produces. We can do this as many times as we need to until we become able to stay with the "uncomfortable" Sensations and move around the circle to the Manifestation we desire to see.

So to review.

When we take on a "positive" Thought of something we wish to Experience, if that "positive" Thought was associated with pain in our early childhood, the "positive" Thought produces "uncomfortable" Sensations that we think are "intolerable." In order to get away from those "intolerable" Sensation that we, because or our history, think are dangerous (they really aren't, but our Inner Child thinks they are) we will "protect" ourselves against those Sensations by taking on the opposite Thought as a "protective" Thought. This "protective" Thought will produce more tolerable Sensations, but the result of this "protective" Thought is that we will not have the Experience we were trying to have when we took on the "positive" Thought.

In brief, the ONLY way to break this pattern of taking on a Thought we wish to hold, feeling "uncomfortable" Sensations, Exchanging our "positive" Thought for a "protective" Thought that is the opposite of the Thought we wish to hold, and seeing results we don't want, is to TOLERATE THE "UNCOMFORTABLE" SENSATIONS that the Thought we wish to hold produces. This is the one key to being able to hold the Thoughts we wish to hold and have the Experiences we wish to have.

The following exercises will teach you to do this.

31

EXERCISE 15
We Can Think Any Thought

All Thoughts are available to us at all times, no matter what is happening and no matter how we feel. You don't have to believe a Thought to be able to think it.

Close your eyes.

Notice your Thoughts, whatever they are. They may be changing moment to moment. You may like or not like what you're thinking. It doesn't matter. Just spend a few moments noticing your Thoughts.

Now think of a pink elephant. See it in your mind. Now think of yourself as having a billion dollars. Now picture yourself doing the Twist on the rings of Saturn.

Logic may tell you that it's impossible to do the Twist on the rings of Saturn because the rings are made of gas and you can't breathe in Space, but you can still picture yourself doing it. You can still think it. Thinking an "impossible" Thought is invariably the first step to eventually having something that seems, at first, "impossible" actually appear. Think of all the things that several hundred years ago would have been deemed "impossible." Television, space flight, telephones, cars. The list goes on. At some point, someone thought of them as "possible." In fact, in our unlimited Universe, EVERYTHING is possible. The first step to "Realizing" something in the Manifested world is to take on the Thought.

Now play with thinking whatever Thoughts you want to think, whether you think they're "impossible" or not. Just think them. Throughout your day, practice "daydreaming" by thinking whatever Thoughts you choose to think, no matter what's happening at the time.

EXERCISE 16
Experiencing Events as Merely a Mirror of What You're Thinking

Close your eyes.

Think of an Event. It can be one that you're happy about. It can be one that you're upset about. Just pick an Event.

As you think of the Event, see if you can notice that the Event is not "happening" inside you. Only your Thought is, and of course, the Sensations that go with your Thought. See if you can Experience that the ONLY way you ever Experience an event is in your own Thoughts. So all you ever "see" when you "see" an event, is your own Thoughts.

EXERCISE 17
Following the Pencil

This Exercise demonstrates where the real cause of what you see in the world is.

It needs to be done with a partner.

Find a partner and stand so that the two of you are facing each other about 5 feet apart.

Take two identical objects, they can be pens or pencils or straws, just as long as they are identical.

Give one to your partner and keep one for yourself.

Designate your partner as the mirror and yourself as your Thoughts.

Hold up your object, and have your partner hold up his

or her object directly across from your object, as though reflecting you in a mirror.

Tell your partner to do whatever it is you do with your object, even if you do something unexpected.

Begin to move your object, up and down, around in a circle, sideways. Notice that the "mirror" opposite you automatically reflects what you're doing without any effort on your part. If it's happening on your side, it's happening on the mirror side.

Contemplate for a moment that the whole motivation for what's "happening" in the "world" in front of you is on your side, and that you need do nothing but do whatever you do on your side to have it be reflected in the "Mirror of the World."

Now you're going to do something unexpected. You are going to drop the pencil. Notice that the second you drop the pencil, the reflection of the pencil disappears from the "Mirror of the world," as your partner, "reflecting you exactly," drops the pencil.

Think about the idea that as long as we hold in mind what we want to see in the world, the "Mirror of the World" MUST reflect it. It can't not reflect it. A mirror has no choice. It doesn't think. It just reflects. The moment we mistakenly think that it is the world that is causing things and look to the world instead of holding the Thought in our mind, the object we're looking for disappears. If we want to get it back, all we have to do is "pick it up" in our mind.

EXERCISE 18
Exchanging Your Thoughts Around a Particular Event

Close your eyes.

Think about an "upsetting" Event. It can be something that happened to you, something that's happening now, or something you're worried about in the future. Doesn't matter. Just choose an "upsetting" Event.

Notice your Thought about the Event.

Now choose a different Thought about the same Event. (You don't have to believe the Thought. Just choose it and think it.)

Now choose a different Thought about the same Event.

And another.

And another.

Notice that you don't get to choose the Event, but you do get to choose the Thought you have about it. Of course, different Thoughts may come with different levels of "discomfort." But if you can be with that "discomfort," you can choose ANY Thought about ANY event. In other words, all it takes to hold any Thought is to be able to be with any Sensations that arise when you think that Thought.

EXERCISE 19
Thoughts Generate Sensations

Close your eyes.

Notice the Thought you're thinking right now, whatever it is.

Now notice the Sensations you're having in your body. By Sensations, I mean Experiences like Pain, Tingling, Tightness, Hotness, Tension, Relaxation, Itching, Throbbing (not what's throbbing itself but the sensation it generates - for example, it's not the fact that your heart is beating, but rather what it feels like when your heart beats).

Make sure that you're describing Sensations, not your Thoughts about your Sensations. "It feels like my head is going to explode" is not a Sensation. It's a Thought about a Tightness in your temples. Focus on just Experiencing the Tightness, not on what you think is going to happen if you do or what you think is causing the Tightness. Just Experience the Tightness.

If you can, don't even give the Sensations a name. Just sit there and Experience them.

EXERCISE 20
"Positive" Thoughts Often Generate "Uncomfortable" Sensations

Close your eyes.

Take on a "positive" Thought that you have been afraid to take on or have felt "uncomfortable" taking on. It can be a Thought that you have something you've always wanted, or that a situation in the future that you've been afraid of is going to have a "positive" outcome.

Notice the Sensations that arise when you think that "positive" Thought. Especially look for where you might be feeling Sensations that you might call "uncomfortable."

Now take on another "positive" Thought and notice the Sensations that one brings up.

See if you can stay with your "positive" Thoughts while Experiencing the "uncomfortable" Sensations that come with them.

EXERCISE 21
Recognizing "Protective" Thoughts

Find a "positive" Thought that you've had trouble staying with. It could be some big dream that has been, so far, unmanifested, a relationship you'd like to have that you've always thought you'll never have, an amount of money, an achievement. Think big.

Think that "positive" Thought and notice any "uncomfortable" Sensations that come up. (There should be quite a few of them if this is truly a big dream that has eluded you.)

Notice that almost immediately a Thought that is the opposite of your "positive" Thought comes up in your mind.

This is a "protective" Thought which your Inner Child, due to some long-ago traumatic event or events, took on to get you away from the "uncomfortable" (and to the Inner Child, "intolerable") Sensations that arose when you dared to think the Thought you wanted to think.

Think the "protective" Thought and notice if your Sensations change. Do they ease up? Do they stay the same? There are no right answers here. Just notice.

EXERCISE 22
The Results of "Protective" Thoughts

Close your eyes.

Think a "positive" Thought that's challenging for you to think.

Notice any "uncomfortable" Sensations that arise when you think that "positive" Thought.

Notice the "protective" Thought (usually the opposite of the "positive" Thought) that jumps into your mind.

Stay with the "protective" Thought.

Notice that although you may be unhappy about the "protective" Thought, you are somehow more "comfortable" with the Sensations the "protective" Thought produces.

Notice that because of this, you are able to stay with the "protective" Thought more easily than you could the "positive" Thought.

See if you can notice that as a result of your thinking the "protective" Thought, you now believe that the "protective" Thought is "true." The "protective" Thought has become a "Belief," which, in Thought Exchange, we define as "A thought that we think is true."

See if you can notice that you are now viewing the world and the possibilities contained in it through the lens of your "negative" Belief.

EXERCISE 23
The Triangle
"Positive" Thought/"Uncomfortable" Sensations/
"Protective" Thought

Close your eyes.

Think your "positive" Thought that you've had trouble staying with.

Notice the "uncomfortable" Sensations that arise when you think that "positive" Thought.

Notice the "protective" Thought that arises when you are thinking your "positive" Thought and experiencing the "uncomfortable" Sensations that go with it.

This time, whenever you notice the "protective" Thought, immediately Exchange it for the original "positive" Thought.

Notice that the minute you do this, you Experience the "uncomfortable" Sensation again, and are back at the "protective" Thought. No worries. Every time you hit the "protective" Thought, immediately Exchange it for the "positive" Thought and go back around the Triangle.

Open your eyes.
The triangle looks like this.

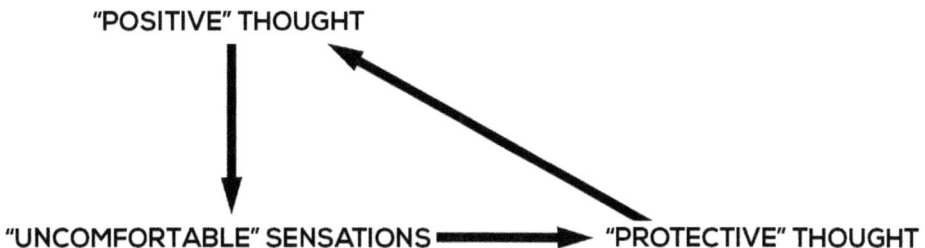

"POSITIVE" THOUGHT

"UNCOMFORTABLE" SENSATIONS ➡ **"PROTECTIVE" THOUGHT**

EXERCISE 24
Sensations - The Point of Choice

Close your eyes.

Think a "positive" Thought that has been difficult to think.

Feel the "uncomfortable" Sensations that arise when you think that "positive" Thought.

See if you can just stay with the "uncomfortable" Sensations without jumping away from them to a "protective" Thought.

This takes practice. Throughout the next few days, practice Noticing and being with your Sensations without trying to get away from them, without trying to "feel better" and without making up a story about them. Get used to Experiencing Sensations as Sensations, with no meaning added.

THIS IS THE KEY TO WORKING WITH THOUGHT EXCHANGE. IT IS THE KEY TO YOUR BEING ABLE TO CHOOSE ANY THOUGHT YOU WISH TO CHOOSE.
IT IS THE KEY TO YOUR FREEDOM, PEACE OF MIND, AND POWER TO SEE YOUR DREAMS MANIFEST.

EXERCISE 25
Moving Around The Thought Exchange Circle With Your "Positive" Thoughts

Take on a "positive" Thought that has been difficult for you to take on.

Notice and stay with any "uncomfortable" Sensations the "positive" Thought generates.

Continue to hold the "positive" Thought and be with the "uncomfortable" Sensations.

See if you can Notice that as you do this, the "positive" Thought becomes a Belief. (A Thought you think is "true.")

See if you can become used to the fact that this particular "positive" Belief comes with these particular "uncomfortable" Sensations.

Don't give meaning or story to the "uncomfortable" Sensations. Just experience them while holding the "positive" Belief.

Practice holding your "positive" Belief throughout the week, doing your best to accept the "discomfort" that comes with it.

Notice what you "see" in the world when you do this. Don't try to make something happen in the world. Just notice what you "see."

EXERCISE 26
Experiencing the World as a Mirror of Your Beliefs

Hold your "positive" Belief, and be with whatever "uncomfortable" Sensations arise when you do this.

Look at the "results" you're seeing in the world, and see if you can see these results, whatever they are, in the framework of the "positive" Belief you're holding.

See if you can notice that a particular result is intrinsically meaningless. What you Believe is the ONLY important part of the equation, because it's the ONLY thing that's happening inside of you.

EXERCISE 27
Changing a Belief

Close your eyes.

Choose a "negative" Belief that you hold. (Examples of "negative" Beliefs are Beliefs like, "It's impossible for me to ever have anything; Everyone is against me; That can't possibly happen.")

Notice that you think you can't change your "negative" Belief, because you think it's true.

See if you can notice that your Belief is a Thought. (It's just one that you happen to think is true, but that doesn't make it any truer than any other Thought.)

Now that you know that your Belief is a Thought, Exchange it for a Thought you wish to take on.

You will, most likely, immediately encounter "uncomfortable" Sensations.

Stay with those "uncomfortable" Sensations and your New Thought will become your New Belief. (A New Thought that you now think is true.)

Notice how the way you see the world shifts as you continue to hold this New Belief.

EXERCISE 28
The Ultimate Thought Exchange Exercise

If you do just ONE Thought Exchange Exercise, do this one. The Entire Key to Thought Exchange, to being able to hold the Thoughts you wish to hold and thus have the life Experience you wish to have, is contained in this simple (but not always easy to do) Exercise.

When in doubt, GO TO YOUR SENSATIONS. Don't go to the story. Don't go to "protective" Thoughts. Don't go to analyzing or figuring out. Don't go to Affirmations or "Positive Thinking." Just GO TO YOUR SENSATIONS and STAY WITH THEM! All that you need to know, all that you need to heal, all the Divine Ideas, all the Truths, will spontaneously come to you out of that state.

So, whether you believe it or not, whenever you don't know what to do, Pause, Notice your Sensations and simply Experience them. You may watch lots of Thoughts float by, you may be tempted to take on "protective" Thoughts, you may feel you need to take action to get away from the "uncomfortable" Sensations.

DON'T.

STAY WITH YOUR SENSATIONS. The rest will take care of itself. You'll know what to do, and the Infinite Universe of Possibilities will open to you, because you will be able to take on any Thought, any time, no matter what is happening.

GO TO YOUR SENSATIONS!

For more detailed information on the subject of "The Technique of Thought Exchange," please refer to:
The Thought Exchange, pgs. 47-124, 157-250
The Healing Power of "Negative" Thoughts and "Uncomfortable" Sensations, pgs. 13-20.

PART IV
MANIFESTATION

I can't emphasize strongly enough that Manifestation is not the point. The point is what is going on inside of us.

But that being said, Manifestation does have its uses, as a mirror that reflects back to us what we're Thinking and Believing so we can see it and work with it inside of ourselves. If we can remember that Manifesting things in the physical world is a "game" we play to exercise our ability to choose our Thoughts, stay with the Sensations those Thoughts produce and thus choose the Beliefs in which we wish to live, only then can we truly enjoy the fruits of the Manifestations that appear before us in the Physical World. (Let me just add here that the Physical World is not the Real World. The REAL World is the internal world of our Thoughts and Sensations, since the ONLY place we live, and the ONLY place in which we Experience anything is inside ourselves in the form of Thoughts and Sensations, Observed, Noticed and Experienced by who we REALLY are: a non-physical, located-nowhere, Invisible Observer/Noticer/Experiencer.

With all this in mind, here are some ways in which Manifestation of what we'd like to see in the world can be achieved and used for the purpose of our interior Wholeness and Experience of Contentment, Power and Peace.

EXERCISE 29
Identifying What You REALLY Want

Before we get to the "game" of Manifesting "stuff" in the physical world, it's important to know why we're playing that game. Since we ONLY experience things in our internal world, NEVER in the "outside" world, it's important to know what it is we REALLY want, INSIDE, when we're trying to Manifest something on the "outside." This Exercise will help you determine that.

Close your eyes.

Think of something you want to Manifest.

Ask yourself, "Why do I want to Manifest this particular thing?"

So let's say the thing you want to Manifest is money. (Substitute your own desired Manifestation in this part of the Exercise.

Let's say your answer is, "I want money because I want to be able to have the things that money can buy."

Ask yourself, "Why do I want to have the things that money can buy?"

Your answer might be,"Because I want to feel unlimited."

Notice that you are already unlimited. So you already have the thing that you REALLY wanted in the first place.

If you're not aware that you already have what you wanted, keep asking the question, "Why do I want this?"

You will eventually get down to something like, "I want to be happy, I want to feel safe, I want to feel powerful."

All these are qualities that ONLY exist inside and have nothing to do with external Manifestations.

So, to review the Exercise in a way in which you can customize it for yourself:

Choose something you'd like to Manifest.

Ask yourself why you want that particular Manifestation.

When you get an answer, ask yourself, "Why do I want that?"

When you get an answer to that question, ask yourself, "Why do I want that?"

Keep going until it pares down to a basic, interior Experience that you are aware is already available to you.

The paradox is, since the world is a mirror of your Thoughts, Manifestation being nothing more than a reflection of the Thoughts you're having, you will not be able to see what you want to Manifest until you know you already have it inside.

EXERCISE 30
Searching "The Great Unmanifested"

All Manifestation begins in "The Great Unmanifested" because Everything ALWAYS existed, ALWAYS exists, and ALWAYS will exist in the invisible, unlimited world of Possibility. Things that we see in the physical world are just temporary Manifestations of a small percentage of the Infinite Possible Manifestations that MUST exist in "The Great Unmanifest-

ed." Every invention, every song, every piece of literature, every amount of money already exists, always has and always will, in "The Great Unmanifested." So when you're looking for something that you don't see in the physical world, look in the invisible world of "The Great Unmanifested." No matter what it is, no matter how far-fetched, no matter how impossible it might seem, it MUST be there.

Close your eyes.

Envision "The Great Unmanifested," a place where EVERY-THING exists in potential form. You can envision it any way you like; as a circle; as the entire universe; as a box; as a room; as a cave. Whatever. Just envision the place that contains EVERYTHING.

Think about a Grandfather Clock. Look for it in "The Great Unmanifested." It MUST be there. Find it.

Now think about a penny. Look for it in "The Great Unmanifested." It MUST be there. Find it.

Now think about a billion dollars in thousand dollar bills. Look for it in "The Great Unmanifested." It MUST be there. Find it.

Now think about your wildest dream, whatever it is. Look for it in "The Great Unmanifested." It MUST be there. Find it.

Throughout the day, whenever you have a Thought of something you want, go to "The Great Unmanifested" and find it there.

Anything you could ever desire is already "There." Which means, "It's already HERE!" Because "The Great Unmanifested" is not something that's "There." It's "Here." In fact, you are a part of it. Like everyone and everything else, that's where you came from, that's where you will return to when your personal Manifestation is over, and that's where you will exist eternally. You can't not, because the Possibility of You cannot not exist.

EXERCISE 31
Merging With What You Desire to Manifest

Close your eyes.

Think of something you desire to see Manifested.

Go into "The Great Unmanifested" and find it there.

Now, either walk over to it or see it moving toward you, until you occupy the EXACT same space as the object you desire. (In "The Great Unmanifested" you can do this, since this is not a physical place, and as such, two things can be in the exact same imaginary location at the same time.

When you've got a good sense that you and the object of your desire are in the same place, open your eyes.

Spend the next few days walking around Experiencing that you and the object of your desire are occupying the exact same space. See what happens when you do this.

EXERCISE 32
Internalizing "The Great Unmanifested"

Close your eyes.

Picture "The Great Unmanifested," however you see it.

Now, take the entire "Great Unmanifested" and put it inside yourself. If you see it as a room, put that room inside yourself. If you see it as a circle, put that circle inside yourself. If you see it as the entire Universe, put that entire Universe inside yourself.

When you've got "The Great Unmanifested" firmly inside yourself, open your eyes.

For the next few days (or preferably from now on, for the rest of Eternity) walk around thinking of "The Great Unmanifested" as inside of you, with everything it contains already being a part of you. Watch what happens.

EXERCISE 33
The Law of Noticing

In Thought Exchange, we refer to The Law of Attraction as The Law of Noticing, because, in Truth, we are not "attracting" anything. Everything is already Here!

Close your eyes.

Think about something you desire to see in the Manifested world.

Locate "The Great Unmanifested" inside of yourself.

Find what you're looking for in "The Great Unmanifested."

Notice that what you're looking for is Never "out there" but Always "in here," in "The Great Unmanifested" that is inside of You.

There is nothing to attract. Everything is HERE.

It's sort of like when an expectant mother is standing in the room with you and says, "The baby is coming." The baby isn't "Coming." The baby is "Here," in this room, inside the mother. The baby will be revealed, but it's already Here.

EXERCISE 34
The Part That Knows

Now that you've done the previous few Exercises, you know that you have a part of you that contains Everything. ALL Possibilities, ALL Answers, ALL Actions, ALL Solutions and ALL Manifestations.

For the next few days, any time you hit a snag in your Manifestation, any time a Circumstance arises where you feel like you're being thwarted or you don't know what to do, simply pause for a minute and KNOW that inside you, ALL the answers MUST exist. Don't try to figure out what they are. Just KNOW this and see what happens.

EXERCISE 35
Accessing The "Part that Knows"

From practicing the previous Exercise, you now KNOW that there is a part of you, inside of you, that KNOWS everything. The thing about this part is that it cannot be controlled or accessed directly. It functions on its own. In Christian terms, statements like, "It is not I but the Father within who does the work" can be translated to mean, "It is not my ego/conscious self that does the manifesting, it's "The Great Unmanifested," the part that knows everything, that does the work.

As such, that part can only be called upon, it cannot be controlled.

For the next few days, expand on the previous Exercise in which you simply KNOW that there is a part of you that has every solution, and actually, in your Thoughts, call upon that part to do its work. Don't try to do the work, don't try to figure it out, just say, "Great Unmanifested," or "Higher Power," or "Spirit Within Me," or whatever you wish to call it.....handle this.

EXERCISE 36
Trusting The "Part of Us That Knows"

One of the problems we often have in allowing the "Part of Us That Knows" to do its work is that since we don't know how it works and can't control it, it can create very "uncomfortable" Sensations in us when we give over to it.

This Exercise gets you in touch with how this part functions without your conscious knowledge or "help."

Make a list of all the things you can think of in your body and in your world that function perfectly without your conscious control. Your heart beating, your blood flowing, your glands secreting hormones, your organs functioning, your digestion, the sun coming up, the tides coming in and out. In fact, the whole Universe functions by itself without your controlling it. Spend some time being aware of this, and realizing how you trust so many of these things without thinking about them.

EXERCISE 37
Don't Push Through/Unblock

The Universe truly does function by itself, and "The Great Unmanifested" within you truly does have all the answers. But those answers are inaccessible to us if we block them by refusing to trust them, by being afraid to open up to them, or by insisting on controlling or using conscious processes to "make things happen."

When you hit a road block in your Manifestation and have become aware that there is a part of you that KNOWS, rather than expending any energy on trying to figure out how that part works or on how the solution will come about, look and see where you may be blocking the flow of "The Great Unmanifested" into your awareness with something you are holding onto, doing or trying to figure out, and STOP DOING THAT. Just as in singing, where if the air (which flows naturally by itself) isn't flowing, we don't try to make it flow, but rather look for where we are getting in the way of the flow, look and see where you are trying to solve a "Problem" consciously, where you are gripping, where you are "in the way," and get out of the way. Without knowing what's going to happen. Without having any answers.

We don't have to make "The Part That Knows" work. But we do have to allow it to work by not interfering with it.

EXERCISE 38
Who are You Praying To?

In religious Thought, God is usually defined as that which Knows everything, has all power, sees everything and IS Love, Omnipotence, Omnipresence and Wisdom itself. In Thought Exchange, these exact same words and images could be used to describe "The Great Unmanifested."

So, if God, or "The Great Unmanifested," or whatever your word for that part within you that Knows Everything is, already has all the answers, and all those answers are within you, you are not asking God to give you anything. Every answer and possibility is already here, inside of you. It's all already been given.

If you find yourself praying for something (whatever praying means to you) try turning your focus from asking "God" or "Higher Power" or "The Great Unmanifested" to give you something, to asking YOURSELF to be Willing to open up enough to allow yourself to receive what is already here for you. When you do this, you may feel out of control or feel many "uncomfortable" Sensations, but if you've done the earlier exercises in this book, you will be able to tolerate these, and by doing so, receive what is already yours inside of you. EVERYTHING!

EXERCISE 39
Taking a Sabbath

I grew up Jewish, and my religious relatives always strictly observed the Sabbath from sundown on Friday to sundown on Saturday. In Jewish law, observing the Sabbath meant not only spending the day in prayer, but not doing any sort of work. No cooking, no cleaning, no handling money, no driving, no talking on the phone. It always seemed ridiculous to me. What was the point of all those rituals?

Recently, as I have looked into it, I have come to understand that the idea behind it was, "We have worked all week, done whatever we could think of to bring about the Manifestations we desire, and now we need to take a whole day where we completely step out of the way to let Spirit do its work and bring about the Manifestations we have been looking for.

So, when you've done everything you can, or when you hit a wall in your efforts, STOP. Take a Sabbath. Take a whole day in which you stop trying, stop doing, and know that you are not slacking off, but rather giving "The Great Unmanifested," the "Part That Knows" within you, the chance to do the work that it knows how to do and that you don't know how to do. And if you wish to spend this Sabbath in prayer, try doing the kind of prayer that you learned in Exercise 38. Pray to yourself for the Willingness to get out of the way and let the "Part That Knows" reveal itself to you in its own way.

EXERCISE 40
Handing it Over

So now that you've done Exercises 34-39, whenever you hit a snag in your plans and you don't know what to do, don't do anything. Hand it over to "The Great Unmanifested," the "Part That Knows." From Exercise 34, you know that the "Part That Knows" is inside of you. So simply pass the "Problem" to the unconscious part of yourself that knows Everything, has Unlimited Possibilities at all times, and let it do its work. You will not necessarily receive an answer in words, but if you relax and know that that unconscious part knows, an idea will pop into your head, you will find yourself doing things you never thought of doing, and even things that seem to be outside of you will suddenly appear.

EXERCISE 41
Identifying Resentments

People often look at Forgiveness of Resentments as hocus pocus or as magical thinking. If I just forgive other people, then magically good things will come to me. But if we understand that EVERYTHING is ONLY happening inside of ourselves, we see that the Resentments we're holding are actually an exact reflection of how we think of ourselves and the limitations we're holding for ourselves.

When you find that your path to the Manifestation you want to see seems blocked, instead of focusing your attention on who or what "outside" of you might be in your way, go "inside" and look for any Thoughts You might be having that are getting in the way. As you think of each person or circumstance that you perceive as being in your way, see if you can uncover some Resentment, anger or jealousy that you have toward them or toward others like them. As you uncover each one, write it down on a list.

Once you have the list made, go down it and see if you can notice that by holding and feeling justified in maintaining each Resentment, you are creating a world for YOURSELF in which you deem it OK and righteous to hold those Resentments. And when you do that, it must follow that in your perception it would be OK and righteous for others to hold the same Resentments against you.

This can be a subtle point to truly understand on a deeper level, but see if you can wrap your mind around the idea that the only way to remove the roadblocks that you perceive are in your way (Resentments toward you) is to remove the road blocks that you are putting in the way of others. You create your world for yourself. If you are living in a world where you are resented, look and see where you are creating a world in which Resentments are OK.

When you get this, or even it you don't get it but have done the Exercise, move on to the next exercise to learn what you can do about your Resentments.

EXERCISE 42
Forgiveness

We've all heard that Forgiveness is the way to clear away Resentments, and yet we have so much trouble doing it. In Thought Exchange, we discover that the reason it can be so difficult to do is that we expect that when we Forgive we will feel better. The Truth is, we will usually feel worse!

In this Exercise, go down your list of Resentments. In each case, allow the person or circumstance to be exactly as they are or were. You don't have to like them, you don't have to condone them, just say to yourself, "This is what happened; This is the way it is; This is the way it was." Period! No story, no trying to fix anything or find a way to make it better.

57

When you do this, you will most likely immediately notice that you feel an escalation of "uncomfortable" Sensations. Don't try to calm them or get away from them, as trying to do this will only result in your taking on your old Thoughts of Resentment. Simply be with the "uncomfortable" Sensations. Notice, "My heart is pounding; I have a sinking feeling in my chest; I'm shaking." Whatever it is, just Experience it. Stay with it for as long as it lasts, and whenever it comes back just be with it.

This is the way in which we process Resentments. We Forgive them, not by saying that what happened is OK, but by giving way for the infinite New Thoughts that become available to us only when we don't run from our "uncomfortable" Sensations by creating limiting Thoughts.

This Exercise may take significant and constant practice, as it is counterintuitive to the way many of us have thought about Forgiveness. But if you practice just being with the Sensations behind the Resentments instead of the focusing on the Thoughts and making up stories and excuses, you will find yourself free to think Thoughts of Unlimited Possibility, no matter what the situation.

EXERCISE 43
Exchanging a Thought For Its Opposite

When you're working on Manifesting something and a Thought of lack or difficulty comes up, immediately recognize it as just a Thought, and Exchange it for its opposite.

So if the Thought, "Nobody likes me" comes up, immediately Exchange it for "Everybody likes me." If the Thought, "It's impossible for me to have this" comes up, immediately Exchange it for, "It's totally possible for me to have this."

Do this every time a Thought that is counter to what you want comes up. Don't worry if you have to do it every two minutes. After a while it will become a natural habit and you will find yourself, more and more, Thinking the Thoughts you wish to think, and as a result, Experiencing the world in the context of those Thoughts.

Of course, we must never forget the basic Thought Exchange principle that when we are constantly Exchanging "protective" Thoughts for the "positive" Thoughts we wish to hold, "uncomfortable" Sensations will undoubtedly arise. As we've discussed throughout this book, our ability to choose the Thoughts we wish to hold and to stay with them is directly related to our ability to be with any "uncomfortable" Sensations that arise, not give them meaning, and stay with our "positive" Thoughts.

EXERCISE 44
Not Possible/Possible

When you are working on Manifesting something and an obstacle arises, take out a piece of paper, make two columns, and title the left column, "If it's NOT Possible" and the right column, "If it IS possible." Then write in the left column the action you would take if you KNEW that what you want is NOT Possible, and, in the right column, the action you would take if you KNEW that what you want IS Possible.

Take the Possible action, and wait for the result. If the result opens up the next Possibility, great. If the result leads you to another obstacle, repeat the process, writing in the left column what you would do if what you want is Impossible, and what you would do if what you want is Possible.

Take the Possible action, and keep repeating the process until you see what you want.

(NOTE: Since, in "The Great Unmanifested," everything MUST be Possible, the Limiting Thought that it's NOT Possible is the ONLY thing standing in the way of your being in touch with the Infinite Possibilities that MUST exist at all times. We take on these limiting Thoughts out of fear of being with the Sensations that the Thoughts of Possibility produce. When you take on the Thoughts of Possibility, they may come with "uncomfortable" Sensations. The more you can be with those intrinsically meaningless Sensations, the more you can stay with the Thoughts of Possibility you wish to stay with, and the more you can take actions to support them.)

EXERCISE 45
Making Your Next Move

When you are in the process of Manifesting something, think of a Chessboard.

Put what you want to Manifest in a square near the upper right hand corner of the Chessboard (but not all the way in the corner).

Put where you are right now, wherever that is, in a square near the lower left hand corner of the Chessboard (but not all the way in the corner).

Go to the square where you currently are. Notice that there are 8 possible moves you can make to adjacent squares. Some moves will take you closer to your goal, some further away.

Notice that whatever move you make, whether it brings you closer or further away, there will now be 8 more possible moves you can make.

There will ALWAYS be 8 possible moves you can make, no

matter how far afield you may go. (This imaginary chess-board is actually infinite, so even if you are in what appears to be the corner, there are still ALWAYS an infinite number of possible moves you can make.)

The path to your Manifestation may twist and turn and at times go in what may seem to be the "wrong" direction, but there is ALWAYS a path from where you are to where you want to go.

Keep making the next move, until you arrive at the square where your Dream resides. And remember to feel your Sensations along each step of the way rather than making up Thoughts and Stories about the rightness and wrongness of a particular move. These Sensations will guide you by allowing you to keep Infinite Possible Thoughts available to yourself at all times.

EXERCISE 46
Turning "In the Way" into "On the Way"

When you're holding a Thought or a Goal in Mind, and something happens that seems to be NOT what you want-ed, say to yourself, "On my way to achieving my goal, this happened." So you could say, "On my way to being a mil-lionaire, I lost all my money." Or, "On my way to having my book be a best seller, I was rejected by 50 publishers." Think of any event that happens as "On the way" rather than "In the way."

EXERCISE 47
Root For People You're Jealous Of

When you are being Resentful of someone else's success, you are living in the Consciousness that you can't have that success yourself. By not allowing them their Success, you are, in your Consciousness, not allowing yourself your Success.

Notice someone who has something you're going for. Take on the Thought, "How fantastic! I'm thrilled for them! They deserve it!" When you do this, notice any" uncomfortable" Sensations that arise as you think the Thought. Stay with those "uncomfortable" Sensations. We usually take on Thoughts of Jealousy or Resentment to try to escape the "uncomfortable" Sensations that arise when someone else has a Success that we desire. By staying with the "positive" Thoughts and any "uncomfortable" Sensations that come with those Thoughts, we open the doorway to our own Success.

EXERCISE 48
Congratulate People Who Have What You Want

When you hear about someone getting something that you have been striving for and have been unable to get, especially if you notice a gnawing Resentment arising in you, or Thoughts like, "How come THEY get this and I'M not allowed," try getting on the phone or on Facebook or on Email and congratulating them. (And of course, feel any "uncomfortable" Sensations that arise when you do this.)

Just do it and see what happens.

EXERCISE 49
If THEY Can, I Can

When you see someone having a Success that you want but have not had, say to yourself, "The fact that THEY are having this Success proves that it's possible for ME to have this Success. By thinking this, you are Exchanging your Thought of "I CAN'T have this" for the Thought, "I CAN have this." Within this Thought, EVERY Success you see in others is PROOF that the same Success is possible and available for You.

EXERCISE 50
Give What it Is You Want

When we "want" something, the underlying Thought we're often holding is that it doesn't exist. When we Exchange our Thought and know that it exists, it appears in the "Mirror of the World" before us. The quickest way to prove that something is infinitely available is for us to give it. By doing this, we create an internal world in which this exists, rather than one in which it's lacking. So if you want Money, give Money. If you want Love, give Love. And as we always understand in Thought Exchange, one of the big reasons we don't do this is that it can feel "uncomfortable." The more we develop our ability to feel "uncomfortable" Sensations, the more power we have to choose any Thought and see Anything Manifest.

EXERCISE 51
When Applying For a Job, Ask What You Can Give

So often, when we apply for a job or go to an audition, we go in with a sense of desperation or a sense that we have to convince the person offering the job to "give it to us," because we "need" it. If someone is looking for an employee, they are not looking to do someone a favor. They are look-ing for someone who can help THEM. Next time you go for an interview, walk in with the idea that you are here to help them. Find out what they need. If you can give it to them, offer it to them. If you can't, move on with best wishes. The reason this can be hard to do is because we are letting go of a false sense of control that says that if we push or try or plead or cajole, someone will give us something. So in order to be truly useful to someone (which is ultimately the rea-son someone would hire you) you have to let go of whether or not you're going to get the job and focus on what THEY need.

EXERCISE 52
Go To The Sensations, NEVER The Story

We set a goal by holding a specific Thought and Image in our mind. When something upsetting happens, or when an ob-stacle appears, the first thing that happens is we feel "uncom-fortable" Sensations. Instinctively, we reach for a "protective" Thought to get us away from those "uncomfortable" Sensa-tions. Before we know it we're all involved in a "Story" that tells us we're in danger; Nothing will ever happen; This is like all the other times we've failed," etc. We then begin to take action based on this story, and since we are now holding the Thought that everything is terrible, that is what we see in the world. All because we were afraid to stay with an "uncom-fortable" Sensation that might last two minutes, or even if it lasted longer, has no power to hurt us. The solution to this, and the way to stay on track, is to do this simple exercises.

The next time you hit an obstacle on your way to a goal, Notice whatever Sensations you're having, Go directly to them, and Stay with them for as long as they last. If they move, follow them to the next Sensation and stay with that one as long as it lasts. NEVER go to the Story. As you stay with your Sensations, notice that whether they calm down or not, you become more "comfortable" being with them, and options you never thought of either come to your mind or happen spontaneously without your doing anything.

EXERCISE 53
Don't Think!

When we have to make a call we're afraid to make, we are often stopped by fear of what might happen, what could go wrong, what went wrong in the past, how we think the other person will react, who we think we are (or aren't) in comparison to the other person...the list of fears goes on and on and on.

The next time you have to make a call that you've been putting off for a long time because you're afraid to make it, do the following FOUR steps.

WALK OVER TO THE PHONE
FEEL YOUR SENSATIONS
PICK UP THE PHONE AND DIAL
TALK

Notice that nowhere in there is, "Think about it; Strategize; Go through all the possibilities." Bypass all the "protective" Thoughts and just do it. In this way, you are accessing the part of you that knows what to do. The worst thing that could happen is that you will feel some "uncomfortable" Sensations, (and if you have been doing the Exercises in this book you should be an expert by now in Experiencing "uncomfortable" Sensations and not acting on them.

EXERCISE 54
Exchanging and Reducing Your "Negative" Thoughts

This is an Exercise that I developed during a long period when I was raising money to have a show of mine produced. With nearly every day bringing new crises and disappointments, this Exercise helped me process any historical "negative" Thoughts that became activated, as well as any "protective" Thoughts I might have taken on during the day. I recommend doing it at the end of the day, before bedtime, but any time you notice a "negative" Thought is a good time to do it as well.

On your computer, create a page and title it, "Exchanging and Reducing My "Negative" Thoughts. When you are feeling stressed, write down all the "negative" and "protective" Thoughts you may have taken on in response to the stresses of the day. Especially look for habitual, old Thoughts that refer you back to "other times" where things haven't worked out. Thoughts like, "Here we go again, I'm about to lose everything." Or, "I've seen this one before and I know it turns out badly."

Type the thoughts out in regular size type.

Now, in a list underneath the list of your "negative" and "protective" Thoughts, Exchange each Thought. So if you wrote, "This is impossible," Exchange it for "This is Possible." If you wrote, "I know how this ends, because it's happened so many times before" Exchange it for "There are Infinite Possible outcomes to this situation, no matter how many times it's turned out a certain way before."

When you've Exchanged all your "negative" and "protective" Thoughts, read through the list of New, Exchanged Thoughts you've created. As you read through your list, sit quietly, and Notice and Be With any Sensations you might be having, even if they're "uncomfortable."

When you've done this, highlight your first list (the list of "negative" and "protective" Thoughts, and REDUCE IT TO SIZE 1 TYPE.

In this way, those Thoughts are still there, but they have been minimized to such tiny type that you can't read them. Your New Thoughts, are still perfectly legible and available to read any time you wish.

Now go to sleep and when you wake up, read your list of New Thoughts.

Keep this list going daily, adding any "negative" or "protective" Thoughts to it when they arise, Exchanging them for their opposite, and then Minimizing the "negative" and "protective" Thoughts along with the rest of them.

Of course, be sure to Notice the Sensations you Experience when you read through your list of Exchanged Thoughts.

This is a great way to process "negative" and "protective" Thoughts as they arise, and to keep yourself on track with the Thoughts you wish to hold and the Outcomes you wish to Experience.

EXERCISE 55
7 Simple (though not always easy) Steps to Manifestation

1. When you're in the process of Manifestation, first know that Unlimited Possibilities Exist at Every Moment. What you want MUST be there. It is NOT possible that it is NOT there.

2. Take on the Thought of what you want to see in the world. Think it. Picture it. Write it down. Say it. Whatever makes it

real for you.

3. Step into "The Great Unmanifested" (which is inside your-self), move toward what you want (in your imagination) and occupy the same space as it. You are now picturing the Infinite Possibilities of the Universe inside yourself, and you are standing, in your mind's eye, in the same exact space as that which you wish to Manifest.

4. Be with the Sensations that arise when you do this, no mat-ter how "uncomfortable" they might be.

5. If you notice any Thoughts of lack or limitation arising, know that they are no more than your mind trying to get you away from your "uncomfortable" Sensations. Every time such a Thought arises, simply go back to Experiencing your Sensations.

6. While staying with your Sensations, do whatever comes to your mind to do. Field whatever opportunities come your way in whichever way you are moved to field them.

7. Any time you get stuck or feel blocked, immediately go back to Step 1 and move through the steps again.

For more detailed information on the subject of "Manifes-tation," please refer to:
The Thought Exchange, pgs. 175-250
The Healing Power of Negative Thoughts and Uncomfortable Sensations, pgs. 101-154

PART V
HEALING YOUR INNER CHILD

The reason we often experience "uncomfortable" Sensations when we take on "positive" Thoughts is that we each have an Inner Child in us who had traumatizing or upsetting Experiences related to those "positive" Thoughts.

The simplest example of this would be: If, as a child, when you said, "I can do this!" someone smacked you across the face and said, "No you can't, you stupid idiot," every time you think "I can do this!" you may feel like you're going to be slapped across the face.

People spend their lives trying to either quiet the Inner Child or convince it that it is safe now. It does no good because the Inner Child does not live in the Now. It is, and always will be, living back at the time when the trauma happened. There is no getting rid of, forgetting or changing the trauma. There is only being with the Inner Child as the Adult we are now, so the Inner Child can know that it is heard, seen and held. When we can do this, the memory of the past is still there, but we can function as the Adults that we are in the Present.

The Inner Child contacts us by creating "uncomfortable" Sensations that put us, as Adults, in the same discomfort the Inner Child felt when it Experienced trauma. This puts us, as the present day Adult, in the unique position of being the only one who can truly know what the Inner Child went through, the only one who can contact the Experience of the Inner Child directly, and consequently, the only one who can heal the Inner Child.

The following Exercises are designed to help you to Experience your own Inner Child, so you can give it what it needs and integrate it into your whole personality. Once you can do this, your Adult life is no longer run by the Inner Child, and you are free to pursue your dreams in an Adult manner by being able to tolerate the Sensations of the Inner Child without having to take on "protective" Thoughts.

EXERCISE 56
It's The "Positive Thoughts That Scare The Inner Child

Take on a "positive" Thought, a Thought of something you'd like to see in your life or a way you'd like to be. Sit very still as you think it, and notice the Sensations that arise in your body. If any "uncomfortable" Sensations arise, simply be with them without trying to change them or fix them.

Try on different "positive" Thoughts. Notice if the "positive" Thoughts that relate to your big Dreams or Desires that have eluded you come with more "uncomfortable" Sensations. If they do, see if you can stay with the "positive" Thought AND the "uncomfortable" Sensations at the same time. In this way you are seeing, feeling and hearing your Inner Child, while allowing yourself to differentiate between the Inner Child who is afraid of this "positive" Thought, and the Adult you are now who can hold and act upon the "positive" Thought while holding the Inner Child who is having "uncomfortable" Sensations. By doing this, you are not only able to stay with and move toward your Dreams, but you are bringing your Inner Child along with you and helping the Inner Child to Heal and yourself to become Integrated and Whole.

EXERCISE 57
The Inner Child Sees The Past as the Future

Think a "positive" Thought, notice any "uncomfortable" Sensations you are having, and identify these Sensations as those of the Inner Child. These Sensations may bring up thoughts of fear, dread, worry or anxiety about the Future. The ONLY reason your Inner Child would be worried about the future is because something worrisome already happened in the past. See if you can bring these worry Thoughts back to the past by sitting quietly and noticing any memories and associations that might come up.

EXERCISE 58
What The Inner Child Is Worrying About is Not Happening Now

Think a "positive" Thought. Notice any "uncomfortable" Sensations you may be having. Identify these "uncomfortable" Sensations as the Inner Child's. Notice the "protective" fear Thoughts the Inner Child has taken on. Realizing that these fear Thoughts are actually about the past, bring your mind to the present situation. See if you can get in touch with the fact that the present situation is a new circumstance with Infinite Possible Outcomes, and that what the Inner Child is worried about is NOT happening now. Even if some of the Inner Child's worries seem to be happening in the present, remember that the Inner Child had to face these circumstances as a helpless child, and you are facing them as an Adult.

EXERCISE 59
View Present Incidents as "Messages" from the Inner Child

When something upsetting happens, before you try to fix it or grapple with it, stop and simply Experience the Sensations that the incident generates. Then notice the "protective" Thoughts, the Thoughts of Fear, Anxiety and Upset, that you jump to to try to get away from the "uncomfortable" Sensations. Don't follow those Thoughts. Notice them, but don't entertain them. Every time you have one, return to the Sensations and stay with them. In this way you are Experiencing the level of fear and upset that your Inner Child Experienced, but unlike the Inner Child, you are able to tolerate and be with this. Notice the different choices that become available to you when you do this, and how circumstances seem to resolve themselves.

EXERCISE 60
You Are Always Having Two Reactions

In any encounter with the "outside" world that contains "uncomfortable" Sensations, see if you can notice that there are two "You's" experiencing the situation. Notice that the "uncomfortable" Sensations you're having are the Inner Child's reaction, based on the past, and the Rational Thoughts you're having are your Adult, present self.

Before you respond or take action, make sure you take a little time for your Adult self to be with the Inner Child, by simply being with the "uncomfortable" Sensations. In this way, when you do respond, you will be responding as an Adult, not as a Child. The Inner Child will be safely in the care of your Adult self, and your Adult self is free to function as an Adult.

EXERCISE 61
Having The Inner Child's Reactions
Without Taking Them On

When your Inner Child is having a reaction, do not try to suppress it, change it, placate it or control it. Simply allow your Inner Child to feel what it feels and think what it thinks. But make sure, while you are doing this, that you do not take any of this on as being true for you, in the present, as your Adult self. You are Observing the Inner Child, not Being the Inner Child. This frees your Adult self to function as an Adult while completely allowing the Inner Child to feel what it feels and think what it thinks. This is, in fact, the Healing.

EXERCISE 62
Being With Your Inner Child

This is a good one to do at night when you get into bed, or first thing in the morning.

Lie in bed and say to your Inner Child, "OK. This is your time. I'm listening. I'm feeling you. I'm with you."

Then just scan your body and quietly be with any Sensations you Experience. Don't do anything about them. Don't try to relax. Don't try to fix anything. You're just giving your Inner Child the chance to communicate freely with you; to feel anything it happens to feel, while in your presence.

Because you don't have anything else to do, you're not under any pressure, nobody is watching, this can be a very powerful Exercise in reconnecting to your Inner Child and any "uncomfortable" Sensations or fearful Thoughts it might have, without judgment on your part. This means Everything to your Inner Child and can be a source of great Healing.

EXERCISE 63
Looking Into Your Inner Child's Eyes

When you're feeling scared or Noticing that your Inner Child is reacting with fear or anxiety to something in the present that you, as an Adult, wouldn't react to in that way, imagine that your Inner Child is in front of you, and you are looking into your Inner Child's eyes. See what's there, empathize with the pain, see the fear and/or sadness, and simply BE with the Inner Child as you would be with another child who was feeling these things. In this way, you separate your Adult self from the Inner Child, and by doing so, are able to hold and help the Inner Child while maintaining your ability to think, feel and act like the Adult you now are.

74

EXERCISE 64
Have Your Inner Child Look Through Your Eyes

When you're feeling anxious or "uncomfortable" in a way that doesn't seem appropriate to your present Adult situation, find the Inner Child inside of you. Locate it in whatever part of your body you are experiencing "uncomfortable" Sensations. That's where the Inner Child is. Picture the Inner Child, and invite it to come up to your head and look out from behind your eyes. In this way, the Inner Child feels protected and can see what the Adult is seeing and doing while knowing that it is not in danger. It's sort of like when a little child hides behind its mother's leg and peeks out. It's looking at the world, but with the protection of its mother who it knows will take care of it. Let your Inner Child experience that same protection by letting it look out safely from behind your Adult eyes. See if you can feel the connection that this relationship creates within you.

EXERCISE 65
10 Steps to Reclaiming Your Power and Passion

Now that you have become acquainted with your Inner Child, are able to hold the Inner Child's Sensations in the arms of your Adult self, and understand, on an Experiential level, that the Inner Child does not live in the Present and as such its Thoughts and Sensations do not limit you in the Present, you are ready to reclaim the Power and Passion that has always been yours but has not been available to you because your Inner Child was too hurt or too afraid to access it. With this Exercise, you can revive unfulfilled Lifelong Dreams you've had, bring Lifelong Desires that have eluded you to fruition, and move through any perceived barriers that have stopped you from achieving your Goals.

1. Think of a pervasive Thought that has been stopping you. Examples of such Thoughts are; "That's not for me;" "I'll never have it;" "I will be stopped;" "Who do I think I am?" etc. Find the one that pops up so often that it just seems like the air you breathe. Like it's "true."

2. Think of an incident that happened to you as a child that caused you to take on that Thought at that time. (When you do this, you will see that it was perfectly understandable and logical for the child to take on the "protective" Thought it took on. It was saving itself from extreme pain and possibly physical danger.)

3. Find the Inner Child inside of you who is thinking that "protective" Thought. Just look in your body and notice where you have an "uncomfortable" Sensation when you think about this Thought. This is where the Inner Child is.

4. Exchange the Thought that has been stopping you for the "positive" Thought that is its opposite. This "positive" Thought will usually escalate the Inner Child's "uncomfortable" Sensations. Just be with them.

5. Take the Inner Child in your two hands and put it out in front of you. I like to think of the child as being like a big chocolate ball with a hard covering that's keeping the softness, the power, the passion, sealed inside. (By taking that Inner Child and putting it outside of yourself, you are physicalizing what is actually happening inside yourself - the Passion and Energy you originally had is being blocked and kept away from you by the "protective" Thought.

6. You now have the Inner Child who was traumatized and is holding the "protective" Thought AND all of your Passion, Power and Excitement that has been suppressed and blocked by that "protective" Thought, in your two hands.

Take that Child (that hard covered chocolate ball, however you see it) and place it right in your heart. (This can be very scary because often you will begin to feel the Terror, Anger, Humiliation, whatever the child felt, in your own body.

7. Hang in there. Feel the Sensations the Child felt. Cry if you cry, feel Pain, just sit there. This is an Adult finally being with the Inner Child, Seeing, Hearing and Feeling it.

8. Take as long as you like, and when you're ready, voice the "positive" Thought that originally caused the incident that made the Inner Child take on the "protective" Thought. You don't have to believe it, you don't have to say it with passion, just say it. (The Inner Child who you are holding in your heart is afraid of that Thought, and this might cause the Inner Child to get more "uncomfortable," but you are holding it, keeping it safe.)

9. When you're ready, let the "chocolate" shell of the "protective" thought burst, and allow all of the tremendous Energy of Passion, Excitement and Power that has been repressed within it burst out and flow through your body. (Whatever your experience is, just have that. I know, in my case, my legs and arms suddenly felt strong and my whole attitude completely changed. I was no longer afraid.)

10. You have now reclaimed the Power that was trapped inside the trauma. Notice how unexpectedly different you feel about things that used to stop you.

For more detailed information on the subject of "Healing Your Inner Child," please refer to:
The Thought Exchange, pgs. 279-306
The Healing Power of Negative Thoughts and Uncomfortable Sensations, pgs. 23-34, 165-288

PART VI
SOLVING "PROBLEMS"

If you've been doing the Exercises in this book up to now, hopefully you understand that it's the "uncomfortable" Sensations that arise when we take on "positive" Thoughts that cause us to reach for "protective," "negative" Thoughts. So it could be said that when we feel the discomfort of thinking "positive" Thoughts, we take on "negative" Thoughts to try and feel more "comfortable." This is the basic paradox of Thought Exchange, and understanding this principle is the key to being able to hold the Thoughts we wish to hold.

Another way of saying this is that when we feel "uncomfortable" Sensations that we don't want to be with, we create a "Problem." We then think that if we could only solve that "Problem" we wouldn't feel "uncomfortable." But the Truth is, if we've put the "Problem" there to try to get away from discomfort, then it follows that when we take the "Problem" away, we will be left with the "uncomfortable" Sensations that we developed the "Problem" to avoid in the first place. It would be like someone who started drinking so they wouldn't feel pain, stopping drinking. Naturally they would feel the pain they tried to cover with the drinking. Recovery would only come when they became able to be with the pain and make different choices around it.

So, with this in mind, can you see that if we were to solve ALL our problems, what we would we be left with is ALL the "uncomfortable" Sensations we were trying to cover. In other words, were we to solve ALL our problems, we would be COMPLETELY "uncomfortable."

At first reading, this sounds terrible, but in fact, if you've been doing these Exercises, you've learned to be "comfortable with being 'uncomfortable.'" That's all you need to be able to do to solve all your "Problems" and be able to choose any Thought you wish to hold and see that Thought Manifest in your life.

So, knowing all this, the following Exercise is a 4 Step process to "Solving" any "Problem" and Healing the Inner Child in the process of doing it. You can use it any time you come across a situation where you wish to hold a "positive" Thought and are experiencing "uncomfortable" Sensations when you do so.

EXERCISE 66
4 Steps to Solving Any "Problem"

Step 1
Truth Meditation

We begin with a Meditation, designed to put you in a position to do this work. In this Meditation, you will move from the Illusion that things are "happening" in the "outside" world to the Experience that, in Truth, EVERYTHING is actually happening in the Invisible World of Experience, which is inside of You.

This Meditation will shift you from focusing on "Solving" the "Problem" in the "outside" world, to being positioned to use ANY "Problem" you see as a gift, which reflects back to you what you need to see and Experience within yourself.

If you've read my first book, *The Thought Exchange – Overcoming Our Resistance to Living a Sensational Life,* you may remember some of this Meditation. But this one takes you further, so stick with it. The whole Meditation should take about 15 minutes.

If you have a recording device, you may want to record the Meditation so you can listen to it in your own voice, with your eyes closed.

If you don't have a recorder handy, you might have someone read the Meditation to you, or if you just want to continue reading the book, read it to yourself and stop and close your eyes when it says "PAUSE."

NOTE: You can also download a recorded copy of this meditation at www.TheThoughtExchange.com.

MEDITATION

Close your eyes and get comfortable.

With your eyes closed, notice the bodily Sensations you're Experiencing. By Sensations, we mean things like Tightness, Hotness, Coldness, Pressure, a "Sinking Feeling," Pounding, Rushing, Tingling, Numbness, Pain."

Sensations are not the same as Thoughts about Sensations. Thoughts like, "I'll never have anything; I feel like my head is going to explode; I'm ashamed; I'm guilty; I'm frustrated," are not Sensations, but rather are our interpretations of what we think Sensations mean, what we think they portend for the future, what we think they say about our past or say about us.

Feelings are also not Sensations. They are, in fact, also Thoughts about Sensations, interpretations of what we think Sensations mean. What we typically call Feelings such as; "I'm happy; I'm sad; I'm angry; I'm in love," are actually Thoughts that are interpretations of what we think our Sensations mean.

What we are looking for here are just the pure Sensations: the Experience of what's going on in our body, not our Thoughts about it.

Sit for a moment and just move your attention around your body, experiencing WHATEVER Sensations you're having. Although one Sensation may first capture your attention, notice if different parts of your body are Experiencing different Sensations. You could be tight in one place and re-laxed in another. You could be Experiencing a pain some-where and no pain somewhere else. There's no right way to do this, there's nothing you're "supposed" to be feeling, nothing you need to change or that needs to be different from what it is. Just NOTICE your Sensations.

We're going to pause for a minute to allow you to do that.

PAUSE FOR A MINUTE

Now, notice your Thoughts. Notice what you're Think-ing. They could be Thoughts about your Sensations. They could seem to have nothing to do with them. They could be Thoughts about the future, or Thoughts about the past. You could be Thinking how bored you are with this Meditation, or how happy you are, or about what you're going to have for lunch tomorrow. It doesn't matter what they are, just notice your Thoughts. Notice if you're having trouble no-ticing your Thoughts, or if they keep changing, or if one or more keeps coming back. Again, there are no right answers here, nothing to change or release or suppress. Just notice whatever Thoughts you're having. We're going to pause for a minute to allow you to do that.

PAUSE

Now, NOTICE WHO'S NOTICING ALL THIS. Notice that there is someone (or something) looking at these Thoughts and Sensations, seeing these Thoughts and Sensations, Ex-periencing these Thoughts and Sensations. See if you can become aware of yourself as NOT these Thoughts and Sen-sations, but as an Invisible Consciousness, located nowhere in the physical world, Noticing Thoughts and Sensations.

This Invisible Consciousness is who you REALLY are. You are nothing (no-thing) located nowhere. You are an invisible Noticer with no opinion (you may notice opinions, but those opinions are not the opinions of the Noticer, they are thoughts that the Noticer is noticing.)

See if you can Experience yourself as this invisible Noticer Noticing Thoughts and Sensations, rather than as the Thoughts and Sensations themselves. We'll pause for a moment to allow you to do this.

PAUSE

So, you are an Invisible Noticer, located nowhere. And as the Invisible Noticer, you have the capacity to Notice anything, to Experience ANY Sensation and to Think ANY Thought. Having one Sensation does not in any way limit your Infinite Possibilities of Experiencing any other Sensation. Having one Thought does not in any way limit your capacity to have any other Thought. You are, essentially, an unlimited empty space in which ANYTHING and EVERYTHING can be Experienced.

Take a minute to be aware of this.

PAUSE

So, now that you're aware that you are an Infinite, Invisible Consciousness within which any and all Sensations and Thoughts can be experienced, let's take a fresh look at those Sensations and Thoughts and see how this knowledge of who we actually are changes how we Experience them.

Go back to Noticing your Sensations. Just Notice the one that first captures your attention, and then look around your body and Notice all the different Sensations you may or may not be having. Again, I remind you, there's no right way to do this. You're just Noticing.

As you're Noticing your Sensations, you may also Notice that Thoughts keep arising. Thoughts about what these Sensations mean, about the Past, about the Future, about what these Sensations will prevent you from doing or cause to happen. This is natural. When you become aware that a Thought has arisen, don't fight it, don't try to change it, don't explore it. Simply Notice the Thought, and then return your attention to your Sensations. The object is not to get rid of those Thoughts or prevent them from happening, just to Notice them whenever they arise, and turn our attention back to our Sensations.

We're going to take a minute for you to practice doing this. Just focus your attention on your Sensations, and no matter how many times Thoughts arise, simply notice them and return to focusing on your Sensations until the next Thought spontaneously arises.

PAUSE FOR A MINUTE

Now, remembering that who you are is the Invisible Noticer Noticing these Sensations, see if you can Experience these Sensations as intrinsically meaningless. If you are just the Observer of these Sensations, they have no ability whatsoever to touch you where you actually live. Experiencing one Sensation does not in any way expand or diminish your ability to Experience other Sensations. Experiencing a Sensation does not in any way change who you are. You don't lose or gain anything in the place where you live, as the Invisible Observer, Noticer, Experiencer, when you Experience a Sensation. It's just a Sensation, being Experienced as a Sensation. Meaningless.

Take a minute and see if you can be with your Sensations and Experience them as Meaningless.

PAUSE

Now, if you're like every other human being on the planet, you probably noticed that as you were Experiencing your Sensations, Thoughts were arising. And these Thoughts may have attributed meaning to the Sensations.

Focus in on one Sensation. Perhaps on the one that first grabbed your attention. Perhaps on the one that seems strongest or most "uncomfortable" at the moment. Just pick one and focus on it.

Notice the Thoughts that arise as you focus on the Sensation. See if you can Experience each Thought as just a Thought. No meaning. Just one out of an infinite number of possible Thoughts that you could be Thinking at this moment. Or to put it more accurately, just one of an infinite number of possible Thoughts that you could be Noticing/ Observing/Experiencing at this moment.

I like to think of these Thoughts as blades of grass that are part of a huge, infinite lawn. When you are thinking a particular Thought, it is one blade of grass. Five Thoughts are five blades of grass. But the lawn is always there and all the other Thoughts exist, right alongside the ones you're having.

Take a moment, be with your Sensations as simply Sensations with no intrinsic meaning, and when Thoughts arise, see if you can Experience them as simply Thoughts which, although they seem to ascribe meaning to your Sensations, in fact, also have no meaning. They are just Thoughts, being Observed by the Noticer that you are.

Take a minute to be with your meaningless Thoughts and Sensations.

PAUSE

So, who You are is an infinite, invisible space, located nowhere, Experiencing meaningless Sensations and Thoughts.

Now, add the "outside" world to this.

Think of something that has "happened" or that is "happening" that is bothering you, that you're struggling with, that you'd like to change.

BRIEF PAUSE

Notice the Sensations you have when you think about it.

BRIEF PAUSE

Notice the Thoughts you have when you think about it.

BRIEF PAUSE

See if you can be aware that the ONLY way you are Experiencing this "thing" that "happened" or is "happening" is that you are having Sensations and Thoughts INSIDE YOURSELF. There is NO Experience that takes place outside of you.

So the only way we EVER Experience anything is by having meaningless Sensations and meaningless Thoughts.

Now, see if you can reconnect with the fact that who you are is the Invisible Observer, Noticer, Experiencer, Experiencing these Sensations and Thoughts. They have absolutely no effect on you. You are constant. You are infinite. Your capacity to Experience can never be either expanded or diminished by Thoughts and Sensations. You are just "Here," Unchanging, Infinite, Invisible, Empty, located Nowhere.

Now remember the "Problem" you picked. State it to yourself.

BRIEF PAUSE

Notice your Sensations and Thoughts.

BRIEF PAUSE

Experience yourself as the Observer to whom those Sensations and Thoughts are meaningless.

BRIEF PAUSE

So, knowing that who you are is an Invisible Observer, Noticer, Experiencer, located Nowhere, Experiencing invisible, meaningless Sensations and Thoughts, which are the ONLY way you ever Experience ANYTHING, even things that seem to be in the physical world, open your eyes.

Step 2
Pick A "Problem," Any "Problem"

Look at your life IN THE PRESENT and see if you can find a Problem. (This is usually the EASY part.)

It can be anything that's making you "uncomfortable," anything that you wish were different. It can be someone who doesn't treat you the way you want to be treated. It can that your career is not going the way you want it to go. It can be that you don't have enough money. It can be that you can't seem to get into a relationship even though you want to be in one. It can be an immediate crisis. Your house just got robbed. Or you were accused of something at work that you didn't do. Or it can be something ongoing, like, you feel "uncomfortable" talking to people, or you always make the wrong choices in the stock market. Pick "any" "Problem." It doesn't have to be your biggest one. It doesn't have to be the most important. ANY "Problem" will do.

Step 3
Don't Fix It. Feel It!

Look at the "Problem" you've chosen.

Now, our natural inclination, when we have a "Problem," is to try to figure out how to get out of it. As Adults, that's what we do. But this time, I'm going to ask you to do something different.

INSTEAD OF TRYING TO FIX YOUR "PROBLEM," SIMPLY GO TO THE SENSATIONS YOU'RE EXPERIENCING.

Think about the "Problem" and just notice any Sensations you're Experiencing in your body. Remember, by Sensations, we mean Tightness, Pounding, Hotness, Coldness, Emptiness, Rushing, Pounding, Pain. Not Fear, Anxiety, Guilt, Shame, Love, Hate, "My head is going to explode" or "I'll never have what I want." Those are Thoughts. We want SENSATIONS. Just notice your SENSATIONS.

Try not to interpret the Sensations. Simply experience them.

They don't have to be big. They don't have to be what you expect. You may find that what you're Experiencing is Resistance to Sensations, the Feeling of Numbness or Nothing, the sense that your insides are trying to move away from them. If the Resistance to Sensations (in the form of moving away, of not Noticing them, or any other form) is what you come across, just be with that. Don't try to push past the Resistance or force yourself to go deeper. JUST BE WITH WHATEVER YOU FIND WHEN YOU GO TO

YOUR BODY TO BE WITH YOUR SENSATIONS.

If you begin to feel overwhelmed, remember that YOU are the Invisible Observer/Noticer/Experiencer, and the Sensations cannot harm you or change you in any way. You're just Noticing them and being with them. Like sitting next to someone who is in pain. You can be with their pain but you are not their pain.

Pause for a minute, and just Experience whatever Sensations you Experience.

Now, you are probably Noticing that Thoughts keep arising as you Experience your Sensations.

You're right on track. This brings us to the next step.

Step 4
When You Come Across Your Inner
Child's "Protective" Thoughts, Think Them!

When we left off at the end of Step 3, you were being with the Sensations that arose when you thought about your "Problem," and noticing that Thoughts were beginning to arise.

When "Protective" or "Negative" Thoughts Arise, THINK THEM.

Don't try to change them. Don't try to correct them. Don't push them away. THINK THEM.

So if, for example, you just asked someone out on a date and they rejected you, Notice the sinking feeling all over the front of your body (or whatever Sensation you happen to be having) and Notice that you're thinking "It's impossible for me to ever meet anyone" (or whatever "protective"

Thought you happen to be thinking).

And just SIT with the SENSATIONS and the THOUGHTS. Have them. Be with them. Allow them.

Be with them for as long as you need to. Go about your day, but every time you notice them, BE WITH THEM.

THIS IS THE HEALING!

Use this 4 step process whenever you encounter a "Problem" you would like to solve. It will leave you free to hold whatever Thoughts you wish to hold, while at the same time, being with and healing your Inner Child.

So, to review the 4 steps to solving any "Problem:"

1. DO THE MEDITATION TO EXPERIENCE THAT WHO YOU ARE IS AN INVISIBLE UNLIMITED NOTICER, OBSERVER, EXPERIENCER

2. PICK A "PROBLEM," ANY "PROBLEM"

3. EXPERIENCE THE SENSATIONS (including the "uncomfortable ones") YOU EXPERIENCE WHEN YOU THINK ABOUT THE "PROBLEM"

4. THINK THE THOUGHTS THAT ARISE (including the "negative" Thoughts) WHILE REMEMBERING THAT WHO YOU REALLY IN AN INVISIBLE, UNLIMITED NOTICER, OBSERVER, EXPERIENCER.

And that's it! "Problem" solved!

Now I can hear some of you saying, "Wait a minute! That didn't solve anything! My "Problem" is still here!

Actually, after doing this 4 Step Process, your "Problem" isn't still here. It's been replaced by an Experience. You are not Resisting that Experience, as you did when you were calling it a "Problem." You are HAVING that Experience. You are EXPERIENCING that Experience. And by doing this, you have expanded your ability to be with "uncomfortable" Sensations. And by doing that, you have reconnected to the Truth that you have the ability to choose ANY Thought, be with any "uncomfortable" Sensations that arise when you think that Thought, and stay with the Thought you wish to hold while Experiencing those "uncomfortable" Sensations.

As I said at the beginning of this section, when you solve a "Problem" what you are left with is the "uncomfortable" Sensations that you created the "Problem" to get away from. Now that you have done the Exercises in this book and have the principles of Thought Exchange at your disposal, you have the ability to be with your "uncomfortable" Sensations and hold whatever Thoughts you wish to hold.

You have no "Problems."

For more detailed information on the subject of "Solving Problems," please refer to:
The Thought Exchange, pgs. 75-90, 175-216, 253-278, 415-416 and
The Healing Power of Negative Thoughts and Uncomfortable Sensations, pgs. 35-80, 119-154, 231-264

PART VII
THE "HIGHER POWER" WITHIN YOU

Underneath all of these "techniques" there is a Spirituality, a deep, meaningful and reliable way in which all of the unlimited riches of the Universe are constantly available to us. We cannot know how this works, but we can know how to open to it, to access it, and to allow it to work for and through us. This has nothing to do with religion or dogma. Call this Force what you will; "The Great Unmanifested," The Universe, God, Spirit, Source, whatever. It is inside of you and it KNOWS everything. If a disease has been created in you, it KNOWS how to uncreate it. If you have an "unsolveable" Problem, it KNOWS how to solve it. It must. It is "The Great Unmanifested" itself, and it is not possible that anything is impossible. Unlimited Possibility MUST always exist, whether we, in any particular moment, know it or not.

Having done the Exercises in this book, you now know:

Your whole life takes place "Inside" in the world of your Experience.

Your Experience is nothing more than Thoughts and Sensations.

Your Sensations do not mean what they did when you were a child, and as such can be Experienced as intrinsically meaningless, without the need to take on "protective" Thoughts to get away from them.

Since you are now able to Experience and stay with "uncomfortable" Sensations, you are free to choose and stay with any Thought you wish to take on.

Unlimited Possibilities exist at all times, in "The Great Unmanifested," which exists within You.

For the sake of this section, I refer to "The Great Unmanifest-

ed" as "Higher Power." Refer to it with whatever term feels right to you.

Here are some Exercises in how to access and get out of the way of the Unlimited Possibilities that this "Higher Power" contains and CANNOT hold back from us, if only we know how to open to them. Access to the Unlimited Substance, Power and Possibility that is available to ALL of us, lies just on the other side of our "uncomfortable" Sensations.

EXERCISE 67
Faith - "Be Still and Know"

The first thing we must be able to do in order to access the Infiniteness that exists inside of us is to be able to KNOW it's there. When you have a "Problem," sit still and KNOW that there MUST be an answer inside you. Don't try to find it, don't try to figure it out, just KNOW. If "uncomfortable" Sensations or "practical," "realistic," "past experience" Thoughts come up as to why this is NOT possible, notice them but do not entertain them. Get used to simply sitting in the KNOWING that Your "Higher Power" is there within you, and to being with any discomfort ("uncomfortable" Sensations) or distractions ("protective" Thoughts) that may arise when you do so.

EXERCISE 68
"Higher Power" Doesn't Respond, It Just IS

Often, when we "pray," we do so asking some Deity to decide whether or not to give us something. In fact, everything is already given, is already here, within our "Higher Power" ("The Great Unmanifested") which is within Ourselves. The issue is not where to find it or how to get it from somewhere or someone else. The issue is how to access it from within Ourselves. The first step to doing this is to KNOW that it is already here and cannot be withheld from us.

95

When you have an issue and you don't know what to do with it, visualize "The Great Unmanifested," the "Higher Power" within yourself where ALL possibilities exist. Just know that it is there. See it. See the solution to your "Problem," even if you don't know what that solution might be. Walk around knowing that the "Problem" is already solved within you.

EXERCISE 69
Get Out of the Way

As we've learned, we do not control our "Higher Power," we do not know how it works, but we can access it by getting out of its way. In this Exercise, when you have a "Problem," find everything that is NOT "Higher Power" and take it out of the equation. If you are gripping muscles, let go of them. If you are taking action, to no avail, to try to stop "uncomfortable" Sensations or control a situation, stop taking that action. If you don't know what to do next, don't do anything. If you are trying to make a decision, let go of trying. Take everything else out of the equation and your "Higher Power," "The Great Unmanifested," the Infiniteness inside you will hand you the answer. Not necessarily in words, but in ideas or spontaneous actions or even occurrences in the "outside" world which you will suddenly be able to notice and use in new ways. You cannot wield or control "Higher Power," but you can (and MUST) get out of its way, trusting that it will come forth with what you need.

EXERCISE 70
Notice 1, Notice 2, Drop it into 3

When you have a crisis, you have three Choices. Notice Choices 1 and 2 and then choose Choice 3.

Notice 1 - The moment a crisis strikes, something upsetting happens, or you are thrown by a decision or a circumstance, look to your left and Notice what your Inner Child is thinking. Thoughts like, "Here we go again; This is where I lose everything; This always happens to me; I can't have it; I'd better give up; Who was I to think I could actually have something good happen?" and on and on. Don't suppress these Thoughts. Don't entertain these Thoughts. Just Notice and Accept that your Inner Child is having them because in the place where it lives, the Past, this is naturally what the Inner Child would think. You are NOT in the Past. So just Notice the Inner Child's reaction, on your left.

Notice 2 - Now look to your right and Notice the part of you that wants to fight, to go into action, to do everything in your power to make what's happening not be happening, to fix it, to change it, to overcome it, to get away from any "uncomfortable" Sensations you might be Experiencing. All of this action almost never works, because it's most-often coming from the scared, hopeless Consciousness of the Inner Child. So notice that you want to take all these actions, but don't take them.

Drop your "Problem" into 3 - Turn to your center, look down into your own heart and solar plexus and body. See "The Great Unmanifested" there. See that this is where your "Higher Power" resides, the "God" part of you if you will, the part that KNOWS all the answers, usually in ways your conscious mind doesn't. Drop your "Problem" into your "Higher Power," and just go about your business, knowing that it is being taken care of in ways you can't imagine, and that solutions will spontaneously come to you, events will happen out of the blue, and ideas and actions will naturally occur to you that you wouldn't have thought of.

This takes practice, guts and Faith, but if you've done the two previous Exercises, you should be able to more and more consistently be able to take the "perceived" risk of handing over all your "Problems." (I put "perceived" in quotes because actually, handing things over to "Higher Power" is the most reliable, trustworthy, dependable thing you can do.) It's like handing over the sun coming up in the morning. You have nothing to do with it, but you can totally, reliably depend on it happening because "Higher Power" is taking care of it.

EXERCISE 71
Surrender

The word "Surrender" often has a "negative" connotation. We think of "Surrender" as giving up, throwing up our hands, throwing in the towel. But in this context, it's nothing like that. It's handing over something that we have NO ability to fix or control to the Infinite part of us that has EVERY ability to deal with it. It's like surrendering your sink problem to the plumber you've trusted for years. Or surrendering the cleaning of your house to a professional cleaning service you've been using for a really long time. You are giving over your "Problems" to an expert you REALLY trust, and you can sit back and relax, knowing that the job will get done better than you could ever do it, without effort, strain or fear on your part.

When you have a "Problem" that you don't know how to handle, sit down, find your image of "Higher Power," whatever that may be, and say, "Higher Power, I Surrender this 'Problem' to you.'" Don't tell your "Higher Power" what to do. (You don't know what it needs to do. It's going to do things that IT knows how to do, and some of them may even seem counterintuitive to you.) Don't tell your "Higher Power" what the result should be. (Since your "Higher Power" is the deepest part of you, it knows what the best result for you would be, in ways that the "conscious" part of you often doesn't. How many times have we wanted a result, it didn't happen, and ultimately we were relieved that we didn't "get what we wanted" because the result turned out so much better.)

EXERCISE 72
"Higher Power" Can

Take a large jar or can and label it "Higher Power" Can. Notice the double meaning. It is a can called "Higher Power," but it also reminds you that when there are things you CAN'T do, "Higher Power" CAN. Every morning, or whenever you have a "Problem," write it on a piece of paper, drop it into the can and say, "Higher Power, I hand this over to you." Then, forget about it and go about your day. Know that the "Problem" is now out of your conscious mind, out of your will, out of your personality, and in the hands of your inner "Higher Power." You don't have to think, you don't have to figure anything out, you don't have to decide what to do. It's all being taken care of by the part of you that KNOWS.

EXERCISE 73
Go With the Flow

Once you have given over a "Problem" or Circumstance to your "Higher Power," assume that WHATEVER is happening is what needs to happen for you to get where you want to go. Often we don't Surrender because there are things that need to happen that we are afraid to have happen. Your internal "Higher Power" will take you there. If you've Surrendered having a great relationship, the first thing that might happen is that your current relationship breaks up. If you've Surrendered your finances, the first thing that might happen is that you lose your current job. Once you've surrendered, assume that EVERYTHING that happens is your "Higher Power" at work, moving you toward you goal in the way it knows, AND YOU DON'T! Be with what is, let go to and embrace whatever Experience you're having, feel any "uncomfortable" Sensations you might be feeling, and KNOW that you are being healed and led where you need to go, no matter how it feels and no matter what you think.

EXERCISE 74
Solid Ground

So many of us spend our lives trying to get Circumstances to be OK, to get to a level of security or health or wealth or happiness, only to find that every time one thing falls into place something else falls out. There is no solid ground to be found in the physical world. It's the nature of this world that it just keeps reflecting to us whatever our Thoughts are, and our Thoughts are ever-changing, ever-evolving. The ONLY Solid Ground exists where there is NO Solid Ground because there is no "solid" and there is no "ground." "The Great Unmanifested," (i.e. our "Higher Power") is the only place where everything is ALWAYS solved, where everything ALWAYS exists, where there is no possibility of us being harmed or losing anything.

In this Exercise, whenever you feel you are not on solid ground or find yourself grasping to hold onto something in the physical world, transfer your attention to your "Higher Power" and to all it contains. Let go, Surrender, have whatever Experience you're having, give up trying to get somewhere or control anything, and live in the Infiniteness that is inside you and that is your birthright.

THE ULTIMATE EXERCISE
Hand it Over

At the end of the section in this book on *The Technique of Thought Exchange* - I boiled everything down to one thing. FEEL YOUR SENSATIONS.

It is this ability to be with our "uncomfortable" Sensations that allows us to be able to hold whatever Thoughts we wish to hold.

And it is both these abilities that allow us to let go to and contact the Source that contains all our Happiness, all our Serenity, all our Solutions and all our Unlimited Possibilities.

So in this Ultimate Exercise, hand every "Problem," every decision, every action over to the "Higher Power" that is within you. Live your Entire Life being out of the way of it. Let your "Higher Power" run your Entire Life and watch your Happiness and Joy blossom and all your Dreams come true. Because, in your Infinite "Higher Power," they all are already true.

For more detailed information on the subject of "Higher Power," please refer to: *The Thought Exchange,* pgs. 150-154

APPENDIX
Thought Exchange Principles in Review

Here's a list of over 100 Thought Exchange principles that have been covered in the Exercises in this book. If you haven't done the Exercises or if you don't have a working knowledge of Thought Exchange from referring to my other two books on the subject; "The Thought Exchange - Overcoming Our Resistance to Living a SENSATIONAL Life," and The Healing Power of 'Negative' Thoughts and 'Uncomfortable' Sensations - Stop Being Afraid of Them and Start Using Them To Heal," a number of these may seem to make no sense. But since you are at this point in the book, and have hopefully done the Exercises as well as referred to the other two books, this list should serve as a quick reminder of the Principles you now understand and that are here for your use. If any of these need more clarification, you can find more detailed and thorough information and explanations in my other two books.

1. There is NOTHING "out there," only inside of Ourselves.

2. There are no "other" people. All "other" people ONLY exist inside of Ourselves, in our world of Experience.

3. Everything that "happens" only happens inside of Ourselves, in the form of Thoughts and Sensations that we Experience.

4. Who we REALLY are is an Invisible Observer/Noticer/Experiencer, located nowhere, Noticing Thoughts and Sensations.

5. Since the Noticer that we REALLY are is located nowhere, it is not "Our" Noticer. It is THE Noticer. This is the place in which we are all One. Everyone is actually located nowhere, and Infinite Possibilities are available to everyone.

6. There is no Future and no Past. They both exist ONLY as Thoughts and Sensations that we Experience in the Present.

7. Your body is NOT You. It is outside of who You REALLY are: an invisible Observer/Noticer/Experiencer located Nowhere. You are looking at your body, Experiencing it via Sensations that are being Observed/Noticed/Experienced by who you REALLY are.

8. Who you REALLY are is ALWAYS safe. It cannot be diminished or expanded by events or by Thoughts and Sensations. You are once removed from Thoughts and Sensations because You are looking at them. They are not who You are. You are twice removed from events because You can ONLY Experience events through Thoughts and Sensations, which are also not You.

9. What happens in the "outside" world only serves as a mirror for You to see what You're thinking.

10. We can think ANY Thought at ANY time. We don't have to believe it, we don't have to feel any certain way, but we have the power to think any Thought at ANY time, no matter what's happening, no matter what the world looks like to us at that moment.

11. Thoughts generate Sensations.

12. It is most often our "positive" Thoughts that generate "uncomfortable" Sensations.

13. If a "positive" Thought became associated with pain or fear in our early childhood, we will often try to jump away from a "positive" Thought when we feel this discomfort, and take on a "protective" Thought, which is its opposite.

14. When we think a "positive" Thought and Experience "uncomfortable" Sensations, we are at the Point of Choice. We can either stay with the "uncomfortable" Sensations and stay with our "positive" Thought, or choose a "protective" Thought to get away from the "uncomfortable" Sensations generated by the "positive" Thought.

15. If we choose to take on a "protective" Thought, that Thought will generate more "tolerable" Sensations, but will lead us to an Experience opposite from the one we were trying to have by taking on the "positive" Thought.

16. If we choose to stay with the "uncomfortable" Sensations generated by the "positive" Thought, we will be able to stay with the "positive" Thought and move on to have it manifest in our Experience.

17. If you notice you've gone to a "protective" Thought and want to get back to your original "positive" Thought, there are two ways to get there. One is simply to return to the Sensation you jumped away from. The other is to Exchange your "protective" Thought for your original "positive" Thought. Either way, you will immediately end up back at the Sensation you jumped away from, and have another crack at staying with it and thus staying with your "positive" Thought.

18. A Thought and a Sensation held at the same time create a Belief

19. A Belief is a Thought that we think is true.

20. Since no Thought is actually true, but is just one of Infinite Possibilities that always exist, a Belief, by its very nature, is a lie. It is taking one possibility out of the Infinite Possible Possibilities and saying that that's the only one that's true.

21. If a Belief serves you (i.e. comes out of a "positive" Thought you wish to hold) keep it. If it doesn't, you can't Exchange a Belief directly for another Belief, because you can't Exchange something that you think is the only thing that's true. In order to Exchange a Belief, you must remember that it is just a Thought. You can then Exchange that Thought for another Thought, sit with the Sensations the New Thought generates, and form a new Belief.

22. What we Experience in the world is nothing more than an exact reflection of the Belief we are holding. Nothing is "happening" in the world. The ONLY place anything is happening is in our Experience, in the form of Thoughts and Sensations that we are Observing.

23. We do not cause things to happen. We see our Beliefs in EVERYTHING that happens. Everyone sees anything that appears to happen only according to their own Beliefs.

24. When you don't like what's happening, look to your Thoughts and Beliefs, not "out there." If you were standing in front of a mirror and didn't like what you saw in the mirror, you would NEVER try to fix the mirror. That would be crazy! It's just as "crazy" to try to fix circumstances "out there" rather than working where the circumstances are really happening: in YOUR Thoughts and Beliefs.

25. You can take on ANY Thought about ANY event, as long as you are willing to Experience the Sensations that arise when you take on that particular Thought.

26. When in doubt, GO TO YOUR SENSATIONS! And stay with them. Don't make up a story. Don't analyze. Just stay with your Sensations and you will have the power to take on ANY thought.

27. Manifestation is NOT the point. The point is what's going on INSIDE of us. Manifestation is just the mirror of that.

28. What you REALLY want is not the "stuff" you are trying to Manifest, but rather the internal Experience that you think that "stuff" will give you.

29. When there is something you want, ask "Why do I want this?" and keep boiling it down until you get to the internal quality that you want to Experience.

30. Since the "stuff" you want can ONLY be a reflection of what you have inside, you cannot have the "stuff" until you have it inside. A mirror cannot reflect something that is not in front of it.

31. When you boil the "stuff" you want down to the real reason you want it, you will discover that you already have what you want, inside of you. The paradox is that you have to know you already have it on the inside to be able to see it on the outside.

32. Everything exists at ALL times, Eternally, in the world of Possibility which, in Thought Exchange, we call "The Great Unmanifested."

33. We don't ATTRACT people, things and circumstances, we become aware of them within ourselves. The "Law of At-

traction" is actually "The Law of Noticing." Find it first in yourself, and it must appear in the "Mirror of the World."

34. Anything that we see in the Physical World is only a temporary Manifestation of something in "The Great Unmanifested." EVERYTHING will eventually go back to its invisible, permanent state, where it remains Eternally, always retaining the Possibility that it could be temporarily Manifested again.

35. In Thought Exchange, we form a picture in our mind of "The Great Unmanifested." Whatever image works for you is fine. It's just a place where EVERYTHING exists.

36. Once we have a picture of "The Great Unmanifested," we move it inside Ourselves so that it's always readily accessible to us. Since "The Great Unmanifested" is non-physical, it can be moved anywhere in our imagination.

37. Since EVERYTHING is in "The Great Unmanifested" at all times, whenever we want to Manifest something, no matter how far-fetched, no matter how impossible it might seem, it MUST be there, so that's where we look for it. Not in the "outside" world, but in the "inside" world.

38. The first thing we do is go into "The Great Unmanifested" in our mind's eye and look for the object we desire. It MUST be there. It can't not be.

39. Once we find what we're looking for, we move toward it or bring it toward us, until we occupy the exact same spot in space as it does. (Since there is no physical space in "The Great Unmanifested," Everything being located Nowhere, we can be in the same space as something else in our Imagination.)

40. Once we are in the same space as that which we want to Manifest, we simply walk around the world aware that it is already in the same space as we are. At some point, depending on how clearly we are willing to see this, it will appear in the "Mirror of the World" before us.

41. If we want to keep something in the mirror, we must keep it in our awareness inside of Ourselves. If we make the mistake of thinking that what's "outside" is causing our Experience, and forget that it's only a reflection of what's inside, the moment we drop it from our inside, it will drop from the "outside," since the "outside" is nothing more than a reflection of what is already inside us. If this happens, don't look for the object on the "outside." Find it on the inside and it will reappear in the "Mirror of the World."

42. There is a part of us that knows EVERYTHING and already contains the way to EVERYTHING we could ever want to Manifest. It doesn't function in our consciousness, it functions in different ways beneath the surface. We cannot wield this part consciously, but we can conjure it up by getting out of its way and letting it do its work the way only it knows how to do it.

43. When we wish to Manifest something, the first step is to know that it MUST already be here, in this place that knows EVERYTHING and in which every possible thing is already contained within us. This first step is to simply be aware that what we want to Manifest is already there, inside us, in "The Great Unmanifested."

44. The part that knows EVERYTHING cannot hold anything back from us. It is not deciding to give or not give things to us, any more than it's not deciding whether or not to run our unconscious bodily functions. It's just there, always available. It is often WE who don't make ourselves available

to IT.

45. We are not asking this part to give us anything. We are not praying to it or beseeching it. We are simply opening to it. So when we are praying for something, we're actually praying to ourselves to open up and let go of our perceived control and preconceived notions enough to allow the Infiniteness that is inside us to come through.

46. If you are having trouble receiving the information you need (which will usually not come as conscious information since that's not how this part works) don't work on how to get it. Work on how to get out of the way of the part of you that already has it and already knows how to bring it into Manifestation.

47. When you have worked and done everything you can, take a Sabbath. Take a day, or whatever time you have, to absolutely do nothing related to what you're trying to Manifest. In this way you give the Part That Knows EVERYTHING a chance to work in ITS way, which is not a way in which you know how to work.

48. When you are trying to Manifest something, if it's not happening, look inside yourself and see where you may be holding Resentments in that area. See if you're jealous of people who have what you want. See if you Resent others who have had success. As long as you're holding these Resentments, you're actually holding them against yourself. Let them go. (To do this you will have to feel the "uncomfortable" Sensations that you took on the Resentments to get away from.) Just feel those Sensations and you will reopen your Infinite Possibilities.

49. One of the things that may be in the way of the Manifestation you desire is a lack of Forgiveness. Forgiveness is allowing things to be exactly as they were, and exactly as they

are now. Since things ONLY occur inside of you, it means that you have to allow your Thoughts and Sensations about a particular person or incident to be exactly as they are. Do not try to change the event or the Thoughts and Sensations. This is the way it was. This is the way it feels. Period. Forgiveness does not necessarily feel good. It often feels extremely "uncomfortable." But by Forgiving (allowing things to be exactly as they are, and your Experience to be exactly as it is) you regain your power to take on any Thought, which is essential to being able to Experience the Manifestations you desire.

50. Root for people you're jealous of. You open up your own path by doing this.

51. Congratulate people who have what you want.

52. Give what it is you want to get.

53. When applying for a job, ask what you can GIVE as opposed to what you can GET. If you give it, you will get it.

54. If you notice that you hit a snag on your path to Manifesting what you want, don't fight the incident. Go to your own mind and see what it is you're thinking. Then Exchange that Thought for it's opposite, and Experience whatever Sensations arise when you do that.

55. When deciding on what action to take next, ask yourself what you would do if you KNEW it was possible to get what you want, and then DO THAT. When you get the next result, whether it's a result you desire or a result that seems to be in the way of what you desire, ask the same question, "What would I do if I KNEW it was possible to get what I want?" and do that. Keep repeating this process until the Manifestation you want appears in your Experience.

56. When you have an objective, some of the things you do and some of the things that happen will seem like they're moving you toward it, and others will seem like they're moving you away. Should something happen that seems like it's moving you away, say, "On my way to my objective, this is what happened." No incident makes it any less possible for you to achieve your objective. The Manifestation you desire to Experience is always there in Infinite Possibility. When you hit a snag, turn the Thought "In the way" to "On the way."

57. When you hit a snag, ALWAYS go to your Sensations, NEVER to the Story. Going to your Sensations will put you right back in touch with your ability to stay with the Thoughts you want to stay with. Going to the Story, trying to figure it out, analyze it or find out "why" something is or isn't happening will send you on a wild goose chase of "protective" Thoughts.

58. When you have something you're afraid to do, DON'T THINK. Just go and do what you have to do, If it's a phone call, just walk over to the phone, pick it up and dial. If it's a book you're writing, just sit down and start writing. Experience your "uncomfortable" Sensations, and JUST DO IT before you have a chance to think yourself out of it.

59. Assume that anything you need to know during the course of your spontaneously doing what you have to do will drop in automatically, since "The Great Unmanifested" within you has all that information, and by not thinking, you are getting out of its way and allowing it to function.

60. Usually, the thing that blocks us from just doing what we need to do to get where we want to go is the trauma and fear that we Experienced in the Past that our Inner Child thinks is in the Present.

61. Each of us has an "Inner Child" who is forever stuck in the Past. If there have been painful experiences that went unheard, unseen and unfelt by a competent Adult, the Inner Child is still stuck in them.

62. Our Inner Child communicates with us by generating Sensations, often "uncomfortable" ones, if it's trying to get our attention about some trauma that went unseen and unprocessed in the Past. By being with our Sensations, we can feel exactly what the Inner Child felt when upsetting incidents occurred. This is the ONLY way in which the Inner Child can heal and stop running our life.

63. We are the ONLY one who can help our Inner Child because we are the ONLY one who can feel exactly what the Inner Child felt.

64. The object is not to change the Inner Child or to tell it everything is OK. What happened to the Inner Child happened and will always have happened. But when we can see, hear, feel and hold the Inner Child, the Inner Child knows that it is loved and that it is safe, and it doesn't need to make us "uncomfortable" or to draw us into circumstances that make us "uncomfortable" in order to get our attention.

65. Once we recognize what is the Inner Child and what is our Adult self, we can function as Adults in the world while taking care of our Inner Child. The Inner Child neither runs our behavior nor needs to be suppressed. We are Integrated.

66. Often, because of our history, and the trauma the Inner Child experienced when it tried to take on "positive" Thoughts, (when it took the initiative and was shot down, when it reached for love and was abused, or when it went for success and the success was taken away from it) it can be the "positive" Thoughts we take on now that cause the most

"uncomfortable" Sensations to arise in us.

67. If the Inner Child thinks it can't tolerate an "uncomfortable" Sensation caused by a Thought, it will jump away from the Sensation by taking on a "protective" Thought that generates a Sensation more tolerable to the Inner Child. The Inner Child is not concerned with our Dreams and Goals. Those are Adult things. It's just concerned with saving itself from pain, as a Child would be. So when the Inner Child jumps to a "protective" Thought, our Adult goals go out the window. At least for the Inner Child. We, as Adults, will have tremendous problems sticking to our "positive" Thoughts and moving toward our goal if we ignore the Inner Child or try to push it out of the way, step around it or over it. We must Experience what the Inner Child Experienced and is still Experiencing, and be able to be with it, so that we can move forward WITH our Inner Child, not IN SPITE of it. We do this by Experiencing and being with the "uncomfortable" Sensations that arise when we take on a "positive" Thought.

68. The Inner Child sees the Past as the Future. It is trying to avoid the pain of the Past that it Experienced when it took on a "positive" Thought long ago and got hurt. It doesn't know that we are now Adults who have many more tools for dealing with challenges.

69. As an Adult, we can know that what the Inner Child is worrying about is not happening Now.

70. The Inner Child communicates with us via "uncomfortable" Sensations that it (and we at the same time because we are in the same body) feel. Those Sensations were not seen and felt at the time of the original trauma, so the Inner Child is still sitting with them. Rather than shrinking from them, we must be with them, letting the Inner Child know that we are with it, are holding it, and, as Adults, have the ability to feel its pain and not get thrown off course.

71. You are always having two reactions to every circumstance. You are having your Adult reaction, and your Inner Child is having it's reaction based on its past traumas.

72. Take care of the Inner Child first. In any challenging interaction, you want to make sure it is You responding as an Adult, rather than the Inner Child responding to the other Adult (or the other Inner Child) from a Child place. So the first thing you must do is feel your Sensations and know that this is the way the Inner Child is communicating its feelings to you. Be with them, hold the Inner Child and then respond to the Circumstances as an Adult.

73. Most marital "Problems" occur because two Inner Children got married, each thinking the other Adult would fix their "Problems." And NO other Adult can fix your Inner Child. Only YOU can heal your Inner Child, since YOU are the ONLY one who can completely be with and understand how your Inner Child feels. The reason for this is that You and your Inner Child live in the same body and as such, Experience EXACTLY the same Sensations and Thoughts. The way the Inner Child heals is that the Adult Experiences the Inner Child's Sensations, holds the Inner Child, and handles the Sensations as only an Adult can.

74. When you are feeling challenged, pause and just be with your "uncomfortable" Sensations (which are the Inner Child's Sensations.) Don't try to fix them or soothe the Inner Child or explain anything. Just be with the Sensations and you are being with and Healing the Inner Child

75. When your Inner Child is upset, sometimes it helps to put the Inner Child in front of you and look into its eyes, seeing whatever upset is there and being with it as you would if you were dealing with an upset child that wasn't you. In this way, you take the Inner Child out of your body and

can maintain your Adult integrity while holding the Inner Child in its upset.

76. In situations that are scary to your Inner Child, another thing you can do is find the Inner Child in your body by going to where the Sensations are "uncomfortable" and, in your mind's eye, bring the Inner Child up to just behind your eyes, so that the Inner Child is looking out of your eyes, protected by you. The Inner Child is watching as you protect it and handle the situation as an Adult, and it gets to feel safe and protected in an "uncomfortable" circumstance.

77. Often, your Power and Passion have been buried inside the frightened Inner Child. By taking the Inner Child into your heart and letting its energy burst forth into your Adult body, where it can be tolerated, contained and used, you can reclaim your old Dreams and Passion.

78. "Problems" are nothing more than what you've created to get away from "uncomfortable" Sensations.

79. The illusion is that once you've solved the "Problem," you will feel fine.

80. In fact, the paradox is that when you solve the "Problem," what you are left with is the "uncomfortable" Sensations you created the "Problem" to get away from.

81. All you have to do to be able to solve your "Problems" is be willing to feel the "uncomfortable" Sensations you'll be left with when you solve them. When you are in this position, no Sensation can stop you from holding whatever "positive" Thoughts you wish to hold, and since life ONLY takes place in the world of our interior Experience, holding the Thought that the "Problem" is solved IS solving the "Problem." When you have the Thought that the "Problem" is solved, the "Problem" IS solved in the ONLY place a "Problem" can ever be solved. Inside of yourself.

82. When you want to solve a "Problem," first get centered in the Experience that who you are is an invisible Observer/Noticer/Experiencer who is looking at the "Problem" "out there" via your Sensations and Thoughts "in here," and that neither of those are you. In this way, you are in no danger, either from the "Problem" or from solving it and being left with the "uncomfortable" Sensations that it was covering.

83. Look at your "Problem" and just Experience it however you Experience it, noticing your Sensations and Thoughts.

84. Don't Fix It. Feel It. Just be with it. Experience it. Don't ruminate on it. Don't think about it. Just be there with it.

85. When you come across your Inner Child's "protective" Thoughts, just think them. Don't refute them. Don't believe them. Don't do anything with them or about them. Just Notice that you're thinking them.

86. Notice that you now no longer have a "Problem." You just have an Experience. You have Thoughts and Sensations that you are looking at from the safety of the infinite, protected Observer/Noticer/Experiencer that You really ARE. It's not hurting you, because you have the ability to Experience it as it is. This is the Healing. Watch what happens to the "Problem."

87. Underneath all these techniques, there is a Spiritual component, a way that the Universe works, a "Higher Power" if you will that contains Infinite Possibility and is infinitely available to us at all times.

88. That "Higher Power" is actually within us, in the form of "The Great Unmanifested" that is always there. It doesn't think, it doesn't withhold or decide whether to give us things. We already have Everything. It's just a matter of our opening up to let our "Higher Power" work.

89. "Higher Power" does not work in the same way as our Conscious Mind. It doesn't necessarily communicate with us through words. It's unconscious. It's the same "Higher Power" that keeps our hearts beating, that runs our digestive system and all the other systems in our body. We don't know how it does it, but certainly we could never figure out how to do those things for ourselves. (And why on Earth would we want to?)

90. The first step to contacting our "Higher Power" is to be still and know it's there. Just to know that it contains every solution and it knows how to accomplish it. It can cure any disease (It created it in the first place, in an effort to bring us some kind of message or healing) and bring any success or insight into our lives. We start by just knowing this.

91. Faith is not wishing and hoping. It's KNOWING that there MUST be a solution to every "Problem." How could there not be? "The Great Unmanifested" contains EVERYTHING. You can prove this by going to "The Great Unmanifested" in your mind and finding WHATEVER you're looking for. It is not possible that there's ANYTHING you can't imagine, because as soon as you think of it, you've imagined it and there it is, in "The Great Unmanifested."

92. When we have a "Problem" we will usually hear and feel our Inner Child's reaction. We will also notice our ego-self's desire to figure it out and do something. If we can just notice these things, drop the "Problem" into our "Higher Power" and let it take it, it works out in ways we couldn't previously imagine.

93. When we worry, try to figure things out, or run from our Sensations, we block our "Higher Power."

94. When we Surrender to our "Higher Power," it's like giving a task to someone who REALLY knows how to do it. We don't have to do it, we don't have to know or worry about how it's going to get done. It is done because it's been given to the "professional" who knows how to do it. We can just sit back and watch, or perhaps, at times, do what we are directed to do by the "professional," knowing that they know what they're doing and we can take the action they suggest with confidence, even if we don't understand it.

95. One tool for Surrendering to our "Higher Power" is to have a jar or a can labeled "Higher Power" Can! Whenever you have a "Problem," simply write it on a piece of paper, drop it into the can and forget about it. It's amazing how ideas and solutions and events will come from "nowhere" to solve our "Problem." (Remember, our "Higher Power" is located "nowhere." It's not physical.) That's because by handing it over, we are allowing a part of ourselves that knows much more than we consciously know to work on the "Problem."

96. Often, the reason we don't allow our "Problems" to be solved is because we are afraid to go through the "fire" that it would take to get to the other side. When we hand a "Problem" over to our "Higher Power," often just the thing we didn't want to have happen, happens. See if you can assume that this is what is necessary for your Healing and your Solution and allow yourself to Experience it, as best you can, without fighting it.

97. Once we have handed the "Problem" over, the next thing to do is go with the flow. Assume that whatever Sensations we're having, even if we're "uncomfortable," are part of our "Higher Power" working on the "Problem." Being able to be with the "uncomfortable" Sensations, rather than running from them, is often the biggest part of our Healing. You can't learn to ride after falling off a horse until you get back

on the horse. Similarly, we can't learn to deal with our former challenges differently until we're back in them.

98. The definition of Love, in Thought Exchange, is allowing things to be Exactly as they are. Allowing circumstances to be Exactly as they are. Allowing our past to be Exactly as it was. Allowing our Sensations to be exactly as they are. Noticing our Thoughts without trying to "overcome" them or make them go away. This ability to Notice Thoughts and Sensations is the key to our being able to choose any Thoughts. A life filled with being with what is, is a life lived in Love.

99. Understand that there is no solid ground to be found in the physical world. We solve one "Problem" and another one arises. We falsely think it's possible that we could solve everything and get to a place of permanent "Peace and Safety." Such a place can NEVER be found in the physical world. But it is ALWAYS with us in the form of our "Higher Power." When we learn, moment to moment, to give life over to our "Higher Power," everything is already solved the minute it comes up, and nothing is a "Problem."

100. So, now that you know that you are an Invisible Observer/Noticer/Experiencer, located Nowhere, only Experiencing life as Thoughts and Sensations, with a "Higher Power" inside you that knows how to handle EVERYTHING, there's just one thing you have to remember. At EVERY moment, give over to your "Higher Power." Live from your "Higher Power." Let your "Higher Power" work. When you do this, you get to Experience your life knowing it's all OK, it's all worked out, Infinite Possibilities are always yours and are available to you. And all the "uncomfortable" Sensations, all the "protective" Thoughts, are just part of it. Nothing to be afraid of. Nothing to fight against. Life becomes interesting. Life becomes fun. Live is lived as what it is. Safe. Interesting. Joyful. Exciting. Full of Love!

101. Feel your Sensations.

102. Give Everything over to "Higher Power" and let it run your life.

For more detailed information on the subject of "Thought Exchange Principles in Review," please refer to:
The Thought Exchange, pgs. 307-42
The Healing Power of Negative Thoughts and Uncomfortable Sensations, pgs. 265-345

AFTERWORD
Putting These Thought Exchange Principles into Practice

Now that you've read through this book and hopefully have tried these Exercises, I wanted to say a few final words about putting them into practice in your daily life.

As I said at the beginning of this book, many of these Exercises can seem counterintuitive, flying in the face of not only what we've been taught throughout our lives, but of what our limited perception tells us is true. In doing these Exercises, we come to understand that much of what we thought was "real" is actually illusion, and much of what we thought of as ephemeral, invisible and secondary is actually real.

In addition, these Exercises often lead us through territory that we have spent our whole lives avoiding. In healing our past and reorienting ourselves to the invisible world in which we truly live our lives and in which all Healing and Happiness can be found, we must walk through all our past hurts and "uncomfortable" Sensations, and learn to work with them in an entirely different way.

Finally, the challenge of these Exercises is that they ask us to live our lives from an entirely different place, to open to and trust invisible forces that seem to work by themselves and over which we have no control in a direct manner. All we have is access to them. It's our job to open to them and get out of their way, but then they do all the work.

All of this can be frightening and disorienting, and doing these Exercises can feel like jumping off a cliff into the unknown. But the rewards, should you choose to, every day, continue to take the leap of practicing Thought Exchange, can be enormous. A life of Contentment, Trust, a new kind of Power and Dreams fulfilled are just a few of the benefits that await us when we are willing to take the perceived risk of practicing these Exercises and these Principles. A new Confidence, call it Faith if you will, that things work out, that everything that happens can be used for good, and that formerly unreachable goals are achievable, can be yours when you understand how things REALLY work, and make yourself available to the unlimited possibilities that are your birthright.

All this being said, practice these principles at your own pace and be patient with yourself. We don't make these kind of shifts overnight. Doing these Exercises whenever you are called to will gradually give you the confidence to let go more and more to getting in touch with the invisible part of you where all the Peace and Power lie, and letting that part, who you REALLY are, work for you. The path can be circuitous. One day we really work the Principles, the next day we get frightened or forget to use them. This is all part of the process. Just keep going, keep taking the risk, and your whole life as you know it will change in ways you never could have imagined.

To support your journey and deepen your understanding of Thought Exchange, I recommend that you read my other two books on the subject. *The Thought Exchange - Overcoming Our Resistance to Living a SENSATIONAL Life,* goes into great detail and will give you all the background you need to fully understand Thought Exchange. And my second book, *The Healing Power of "Negative Thoughts" and "Uncomfortable" Sensations - Stop Being Afraid of Them and Learn To Use Them To Heal,* goes into greater depth on the subjects of being with "uncomfortable" Sensations and understanding our Inner Child.

These books can be found at TheThoughtExchange.com. For those of you who prefer to listen rather than read, they are also available in Audio Book form. In addition, you will find a Documentary there where I talk about Thought Exchange and describe all the basic principles. For those who would like a quick overview in video form, this can be an excellent introduction to the subject.

And finally, for those of you who would like to work with me personally on Thought Exchange, I offer workshops in New York and Connecticut, I speak and teach around the country, and I am available for private sessions. For those of you not in my area, I also do phone sessions. For information on this, you can go to TheThoughtExchange.com. Also, I am always open to receiving your Thoughts and questions by email at TheThoughtExchange@aol.com.

I am happy to have shared this book with you, and am always happy to share Thought Exchange with the world. It has transformed my life, and it is my greatest wish that it do the same for yours.

www.ingramcontent.com/pod-product-compliance
Lightning Source LLC
Chambersburg PA
CBHW071808090426
42737CB00012B/1995